Pearson Revise

T0351596

Pearson Edexcel GCSE (9–1)

Business

Model Answer Workbook

Series Consultant: Harry Smith

Author: Helen Coupland-Smith

Also available to support your revision:

Revise GCSE Study Skills Guide   9781292318875

The **Revise GCSE Study Skills Guide** is full of tried-and-trusted hints and tips for how to learn more effectively. It gives you techniques to help you achieve your best – throughout your GCSE studies and beyond!

Revise GCSE Revision Planner   9781292318868

The **Revise GCSE Revision Planner** helps you to plan and organise your time, step-by-step, throughout your GCSE revision. Use this book and wall chart to mastermind your revision.

For the full range of Pearson revision titles across KS2, 11+, KS3, GCSE, Functional Skills, AS/A Level and BTEC visit: www.pearsonschools.co.uk/revise

Contents

1   Command words

2   Mark schemes

3   How to use this book

4   Paper 1, Section A

16   Paper 1, Section B

31   Paper 1, Section C

39   Paper 2, Section A

57   Paper 2, Section B

69   Paper 2, Section C

76   Answers

About your exam

Your Pearson Edexcel (9–1) Business GCSE comprises **two** exam papers.

Paper 1: Investigating small business ①

Section A 35 marks

Section B 30 marks

Section C 25 marks

Comprising calculations, multiple choice, short answer and extended writing.

Sections B and C are based on business contexts given to you in the extracts in the examination paper.

Content examined 1.1 to 1.5 in the specification.

The paper is...

 written   1 hour 30 minutes   worth 90 marks   % 50% of the total

Paper 2: Building a business ②

Section A 35 marks

Section B 30 marks

Section C 25 marks

Comprising calculations, multiple choice, short answer and extended writing.

Sections B and C are based on business contexts given to you in the extracts in the examination paper.

Content examined 2.1 to 2.5 in the specification.

The paper is...

 written   1 hour 30 minutes   worth 90 marks   % 50% of the total

Pearson Edexcel Business GCSE (9–1) is not tiered. This means that all students will sit the same exam papers and will have access to the full range of grades.

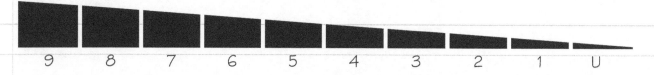

9   8   7   6   5   4   3   2   1   U

A small bit of small print:

Pearson Edexcel publishes Sample Assessment Material and the Specification on its website. This is the official content and this book should be used in conjunction with it. The questions and mark schemes have been written to help you practise every topic in the book. Remember: the real exam questions and mark schemes may not look like this.

Command words

Understanding command words

A command word is the first word in a question. It tells you how you should answer the question. Shown below are the command words used in Pearson Edexcel (9–1) Business GCSE, along with some tips on how to approach each type of question.

Which one or which two
Select the correct answer or answers from a range of possible answers. This is used in multiple choice questions. These questions are testing your ability to recall knowledge.

Define
Write a precise definition of the term stated. It is important not to reuse the words from the term in your definition. These questions are testing your ability to recall knowledge.

Outline
Make a relevant point in context and develop with one further step also in context.

State
Give a short answer. It is important to make sure that your answer is appropriate to the context given.

Identify
Select the correct answer from reading a graph or table of data. Make sure you read the information carefully and express your answer with the correct units, for example £ or %.

Explain
Make a relevant point and develop with two steps. These are generic answers as there is no context to apply your answer to.

Calculate
Carry out a calculation. You must write the formula, input the correct numbers from the data given and express the answer showing the correct units. You may also be asked to complete missing figures in a table.

Analyse
Requires an extended response with a number of steps in a line of reasoning in context, using business terminology as well as specific information from the extract provided. It is important to show balance in your answer. A justified recommendation must be made as to which option has been chosen.

Discuss
Requires an extended response with a number of steps in a line of reasoning, using business terminology. There is no context given; however, you can use your own examples if this helps to demonstrate the point being made.

Evaluate
Requires an extended response with a number of steps in a line of reasoning on context, using business terminology as well as specific information from the extract. Analytical paragraphs should lead to a fully supported conclusion based on the context provided.

Mark schemes

Understanding mark schemes

Mark schemes tell the examiner how to allocate marks to your exam scripts. They are therefore very useful to you as a student. They tell you what the examiner is looking for.

Mark schemes for short answers

This shows what is expected in your answer and therefore what to award marks to.

This gives an example of an acceptable answer.

Answer	Mark
Award 1 mark for identification of a relevant benefit, plus two further marks for development of this benefit up to a total of 3 marks.	
Support from the franchisor (1), meaning that the entrepreneur will be given advice on issues such as cash flow management (1). Therefore, reducing the risk to an inexperienced entrepreneur of failure (1).	(3) AO1a = 1 AO1b = 2

This shows how the marks are split between the exam skills.

Extended answer mark schemes

Extended answers are marked by response level marking. The examiner must first decide in which level to put the answer and then where to place it within that level.

Level	Mark	Descriptor
Level 1	1–3	• Limited application of knowledge and understanding of business concepts and issues to the business context (AO2). • Attempts to deconstruct business information and/or issues, finding limited connections between points (AO3a). • Makes a judgement, providing a simple justification based on limited evaluation of business information and issues relevant to the choice made (AO3b).
Level 2	4–6	• Sound application of knowledge and understanding of business concepts and issues to the business context, although there may be some inconsistencies (AO2). • Deconstructs business information and/or issues, finding interconnected points with chain of reasoning, although there may be some logical inconsistencies (AO3a). • Makes a judgement, providing a justification based on sound evaluation of business information and issues relevant to the choice made (AO3b).
Level 3	7–9	• Detailed application of knowledge and understanding of business concepts and issues to the business context throughout (AO2). • Deconstructs business information and/or issues, finding detailed interconnected points with logical chains of reasoning (AO3a). • Makes a judgement, providing a clear justification based on a thorough evaluation of business information and issues relevant to the choice made (AO3b).

The descriptors show what skills the examiner is looking for at each level. To achieve the full marks available within a level, all of the descriptors at that level must be satisfied.

How to use this book

In this book, you will familiarise yourself with the Pearson Edexcel (9–1) Business GCSE by engaging with exam-style questions, answers and mark schemes. Doing so will mean you know exactly what to expect in the exam and, just as importantly, what will be expected of you.

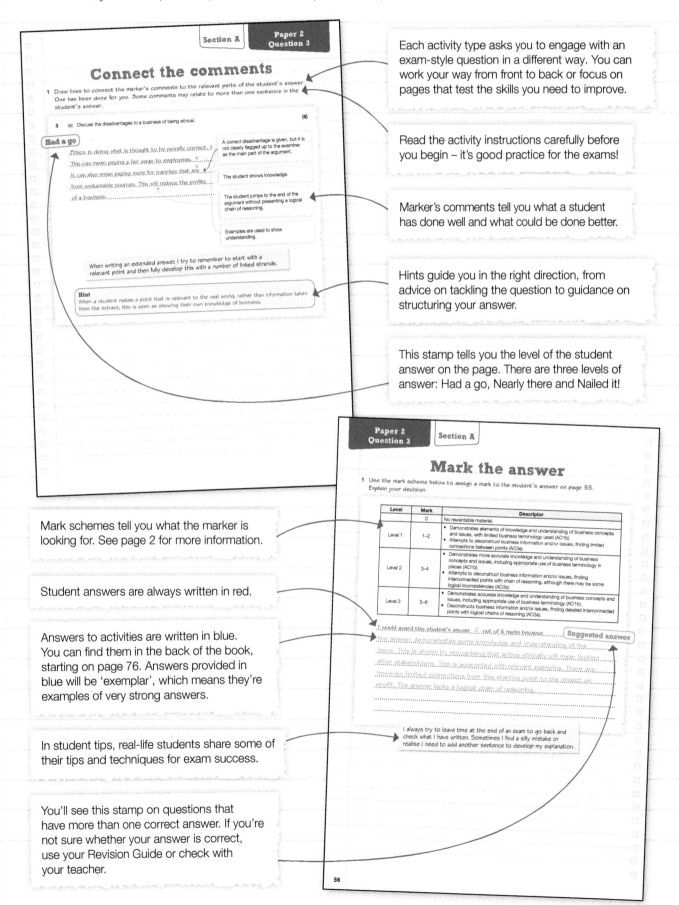

Each activity type asks you to engage with an exam-style question in a different way. You can work your way from front to back or focus on pages that test the skills you need to improve.

Read the activity instructions carefully before you begin – it's good practice for the exams!

Marker's comments tell you what a student has done well and what could be done better.

Hints guide you in the right direction, from advice on tackling the question to guidance on structuring your answer.

This stamp tells you the level of the student answer on the page. There are three levels of answer: Had a go, Nearly there and Nailed it!

Mark schemes tell you what the marker is looking for. See page 2 for more information.

Student answers are always written in red.

Answers to activities are written in blue. You can find them in the back of the book, starting on page 76. Answers provided in blue will be 'exemplar', which means they're examples of very strong answers.

In student tips, real-life students share some of their tips and techniques for exam success.

You'll see this stamp on questions that have more than one correct answer. If you're not sure whether your answer is correct, use your Revision Guide or check with your teacher.

Find the answer

1 Find the answer that would be awarded 1 mark. Choose **A, B, C** or **D**. Explain your choice.

1   (a)   Which **one** of the following is an example of primary market research?
Select **one** answer: **(1)**

☐   **A**   Internet

☐   **B**   Focus group

☐   **C**   Market report

☐   **D**   Government report

Answer .... would be awarded 1 mark because ....

....

....

....

....

....

2 Find the answer that would be awarded 1 mark. Choose **A, B, C** or **D**. Explain your choice.

1   (b)   Which **one** of the following describes stakeholders?
Select **one** answer: **(1)**

☐   **A**   Anyone who is a part owner of a business

☐   **B**   Any individual who has invested finance into a business

☐   **C**   Anyone from outside the business who has an interest in the business

☐   **D**   Anyone who is interested in and potentially affected by the business

Answer .... would be awarded 1 mark because ....

....

....

....

....

Complete the answer

1 Complete the student's answer so it would be awarded 3 marks.

---

1 (c) Explain **one** reward that motivates an entrepreneur when starting a new business. **(3)**

> **Hint**
> One reward has been identified. The question asks you to 'explain' one reward, so now you need to extend the answer to explain the benefit. Try to use two steps in your explanation in order to gain 3 marks in total.

Nearly there

One reward that would motivate an entrepreneur is financial success.
....
....
....
....
....
....
....

---

2 Complete the student's answer so it would be awarded 3 marks.

---

1 (d) Explain **one** disadvantage to an entrepreneur of using loans as a source of finance. **(3)**

> **Hint**
> This time the supporting explanation has been given, so you now need to identify the disadvantage being explained.

Nearly there

....
This is a cost to the entrepreneur every month. As a result, it will be harder for the ....
business to make a profit...
....
....
....
....

> In practice exams I used to always run out of time. Now I realise how important it is to keep answers concise on the short-answer questions at the start of the exam, to ensure I have enough time later for the higher mark questions.

Improve the answer

1 Use the hints below to write an improved answer to this question.

---

1 (c) Explain **one** role of an entrepreneur when setting up a business. **(3)**

> **Hint**
> Remember, for 3-mark 'Explain' questions there is 1 mark for stating a correct point, in this case a role. The further 2 marks are awarded for explaining that point.

> **Hint**
> Use connectives such as 'this means that', 'which will lead to' and 'therefore', etc., to help you develop your explanations.

Had a go

Making business decisions.

....

....

....

....

....

....

....

> I always start my answers with a relevant point or piece of theory from the specification. To help me do this I use the specification when revising.

---

2 Use the hints above to write an improved answer to this question.

---

1 (d) Explain the importance of cash to a business. **(3)**

Nearly there

One reason why cash is important is because it will allow the business to meet

day-to-day expenses. This will allow it to buy new supplies, pay wages

and utility bills.

....

....

....

....

Complete the question

1 Complete the question by adding three multiple choice options. Make sure two are correct.

> **Hint**
> Multiple choice questions often have answers that are believable but incorrect. These are called distractors. Try to make it relatively difficult to spot the incorrect answer.

2   (a) Which **two** of the following are examples of non-financial business objectives?
      Select **two** answers.   **(2)**

☐ **A** Market share

☑ **B** ....

☑ **C** ....

☐ **D** ....

☐ **E** Profit

2 Complete the question by adding three multiple choice options. Make sure two are correct.

2   (b) Which **two** of the following are examples of short-term sources of finance?
      Select **two** answers.   **(2)**

☐ **A** Share capital

☑ **B** ....

☐ **C** ....

☐ **D** Retained profit

☑ **E** ....

Find the answer

1 Find the answer that would be awarded 2 marks. Choose **A**, **B** or **C**. Explain your choice.

Table 1 contains information about a small business for its first year. The business sold 10 000 units in this year.

Fixed costs	£20 000
Variable costs (per unit)	£6.50
Selling price (per unit)	£9.00

Table 1

2 (c) Using the information in **Table 1**, calculate the break-even output
for this business. You are advised to show your workings. (2)

A $\dfrac{10\,000 \text{ units}}{(£9.00 - £6.50)} = \dfrac{10\,000 \text{ units}}{(£2.50)} = 4\,000 \text{ units}$

> I always show my workings, because even if the answer is wrong, I might get some marks.

B $\dfrac{£20\,000}{(£9.00 - £6.50)} = \dfrac{£20\,000}{(£2.50)} = 8\,000 \text{ units}$

Hint
Always check your answer. It is very easy in exam conditions to press a wrong number on your calculator.

C $\dfrac{£9.00 \times 10\,000}{£20\,000} = \dfrac{£90\,000}{£20\,000} = 4\,500 \text{ units}$

Answer .... would be awarded 2 marks because ....

....

2 Find the answer that would be awarded 2 marks. Choose **A**, **B** or **C**. Explain your choice.

Table 2 shows the cash flow forecast for a small business.

2 (c) Complete **Table 2** with the two missing figures. (2)

	Month 1 (£)	Month 2 (£)
Cash inflows	28 500	30 800
Cash outflows	31 000	**(ii)** ....
Net cash flow	**(i)**	3000
Opening balance	5000	2500
Closing balance	2500	5500

Table 2

A i = (2500), ii = 33 800

B i = (2500), ii = 27 800

C i = 2500, ii = 27 800

Answer .... would be awarded 2 marks because ....

....

Improve the answer

1 Use the hints below to write an improved answer to this question.

2 (d) Explain **one** benefit to a new business of starting as a franchise. **(3)**

> **Hint**
> Remember, for 3-mark 'Explain' questions there is 1 mark for stating a correct point, in this case a benefit. The further 2 marks are for explaining this benefit.

Had a go

Support from the franchisor.

....

....

....

....

....

....

I used to just focus on learning advantages and disadvantages. Now I practise developing why each point is an advantage or a disadvantage. This has really helped me gain confidence.

2 Use the hints below to write an improved answer to this question.

2 (e) Explain **one** purpose of producing a business plan. **(3)**

Nearly there

One purpose is it will make it easier for an entrepreneur to obtain finance. This is because it can show a bank manager the forecast cash flow.

....

....

....

....

....

....

....

....

9

Complete the question

1 Complete the question by adding three multiple choice options. Make sure only one is correct.

3   (a)   Which **one** of the following is an advantage of being a private limited company?

Select **one** answer.   **(1)**

     ☐   **A**   Retained profit

     ☑   **B**   ....

     ☐   **C**   ....

     ☐   **D**   ....

2 Complete the question by adding four multiple choice options. Make sure only one is correct.

3   (a)   Which **one** of the following is an example of the impact of technology on the marketing mix?

Select **one** answer.   **(1)**

     ☐   **A**   ....

     ☐   **B**   ....

     ☑   **C**   ....

     ☐   **D**   ....

> **Hint**
> When answering a multiple choice question, is important to read all of the options carefully. The examiner will often include an answer that is quite close to the correct one. If you cross through the answers you know are wrong first, this will help you to narrow down the correct answer.

3 Complete the question by adding four multiple choice options. Make sure only one is correct.

3   (a)   Which one of the following is a type of organisational structure?

Select **one** answer.   **(1)**

     ☐   **A**   ....

     ☑   **B**   ....

     ☐   **C**   ....

     ☐   **D**   ....

Improve the answer

1 Write an improved answer that would be awarded full marks.

Figure 1 shows the change in the profit of a business over three months.

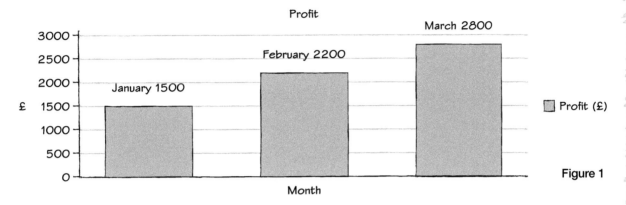

Figure 1

Hint
Remember that the information presented in graphs will be stated on each axis. It is important to read the axis carefully.

3 (b) Using the information in **Figure 1**, calculate the percentage increase in profit between January and March. You are advised to show your workings.

(2)

Hint
When calculating the percentage difference between two numbers, use the percentage change calculation. Remember the formula is: $\frac{change}{original} \times 100$. Don't forget the × 100 to express your answer as a percentage.

$$£2800$$
$$- £1500$$
$$= £1300$$

When I was revising for my exams, I tried all of the 'Calculate' questions over and over again. I would sometimes change the numbers in the question, just so I had new numbers to practise with. I would then ask someone to check my answers for me.

Mark the answer

1 Use the marking instructions below to decide how many marks you would award this student's answer.

---

3 (c) Explain **one** benefit to consumers of consumer law. (3)

Had a go

One benefit of consumer law is that the customer has the right to return goods that are faulty. This means that the customer will not have wasted money. This also means that the business must disclose all information about a product to the customer.

Question	Answer	Mark
3 (c)	Award 1 mark for identification of a benefit, plus 2 further marks for explaining this benefit up to a total of 3 marks. Answers that list more than one benefit with no explanation will be awarded a maximum of 1 mark.	3

I would award this student's answer ..... out of 3 marks because .....

....

....

....

....

....

....

....

....

When I first started practising exam-style questions, I would try and write down everything I knew about a topic. For example, if I had learned four benefits to the consumer of consumer law, I wrote about all of them. Now I have learned to be strict with myself on the lower mark questions and state just one benefit, which I then develop. This approach has saved me a lot of time and improved my marks.

Connect the comments

1 Draw lines to connect the marker's comments to the relevant parts of the student's answer. One has been done for you. Some comments may relate to more than one sentence in the student's answer.

3 (e) Discuss the benefit to a business of understanding customer needs. (6)

> **Hint**
> When answering a 6-mark question, remember to start your answer with a relevant point and then develop it with interconnected strands. Make sure that the strands follow on from each other in a logical order.

Had a go

A business will be able to provide a product that meets the needs of the customer. This will allow the business to make more sales, which will result in greater revenue, so allowing the business to achieve a profit. This will lead to satisfied customers, because the business will provide what they want.

The student makes good use of business terminology.

A correct benefit has been identified, showing accurate knowledge.

However, the logical analysis breaks down, as the next point does not logically follow on from the previous points.

There are a number of connected strands in the student's argument.

To support my revision, I created a set of keyword revision cards – these were especially useful to help learn key business terms that might come up in the exam.

Mark the answer

1 Use the mark scheme below to assign a mark to the student's answer on page 13.
Explain your decision.

Level	Mark	Descriptor
	0	No rewardable material.
Level 1	1–2	• Demonstrates elements of knowledge and understanding of business concepts and issues, with limited business terminology used (AO1b). • Attempts to deconstruct business information and/or issues, finding limited connections between points (AO3a).
Level 2	3–4	• Demonstrates more accurate knowledge and understanding of business concepts and issues, including appropriate use of business terminology in places (AO1b). • Attempts to deconstruct business information and/or issues, finding interconnected points with chain of reasoning, although there may be some logical inconsistencies (AO3a).
Level 3	5–6	• Demonstrates accurate knowledge and understanding of business concepts and issues, including appropriate use of business terminology (AO1b). • Deconstructs business information and/or issues, finding detailed interconnected points with logical chains of reasoning (AO3a).

I would award the student's answer ...... out of 6 marks because ....
....
....
....
....
....
....
....
....
....

Re-order the answer

1 The sentences below are taken from a paragraph written by a student in response to the following question. Rearrange the sentences into the most logical order by numbering them 1 to 7.

3 (e) Discuss the benefits to a business of using e-commerce. (6)

.......This is because there will be no fixed costs for a physical store.........................

.......Therefore, more customers will be able to use the business.............................

.......Therefore, the business will have a lower break-even point..............................

.......Leading to an increase in sales revenue...

.......One benefit of using e-commerce is lower total costs.....................................

.......Another benefit is it will allow the business to reach a larger market..................

.......This means that the business will be able to start making a profit earlier...............

Before I hand my work in to my teacher to mark, I always reread my answer to see if my arguments are logical. If I have time in the exam I will do this as well.

Hint
In 'Discuss' questions, use business terminology within your reasoning.

Case study

Brad is a young entrepreneur who set up Brad Bikes while at university. He was a keen cyclist and realised that there was demand for reasonably priced cycling accessories. At university in Reading he saw a large number of students cycling every day with poor-quality lights, helmets and locks. Brad sourced better-quality accessories from China and sold them via a website he designed and built himself. He soon realised that the amount of profit he could make was only small in relation to the amount of time he was spending on keeping the website up to date and processing orders. He was, however, keen to combine his love of cycling with an online business.

Brad carried out some market research among his friends at university and they all seemed to agree that there was very little cycle wear that they found to be of good quality, functional and fashionable. It is from here that Brad got the idea to set up his own cycle wear brand Moser. It would design and produce a quality product at a reasonable price. His product range would include a wide range of styles and sizes.

In 2017 Brad graduated from university and decided to dedicate all of his time to building his brand Moser. He designed a new website just to sell cycle wear, closing Brad Bikes. He forecast sales revenue of £175 000 in 2019. His brand was starting to gain a solid reputation with amateur cyclists, who generally gave positive reviews on social media. However, the market was becoming increasingly competitive.

> **Hint**
> Underline or highlight the key information in the extract.

Odd one out

1 Use the mark scheme below to decide which of these answers would **not** be awarded 2 marks. Explain your answer.

4 (a) Outline **one** market segment that Brad could target with his brand of cycle wear, Moser. **(2)**

Question	Answer	Mark
4 (a)	Award up to 2 marks for linked points outlining a suitable market segment for Moser. Award a maximum of 1 mark if points are not linked.	2

A People with a healthy lifestyle are a suitable market segment because the cycle wear is designed to be functional when cycling as a sporting activity.

B Teenagers are a market segment because they will want cycle wear that is also fashionable.

C One suitable market segment is parents of students who are studying at university, because they will want their child to have good-quality lights when cycling.

D One suitable market segment is young professionals, because they will want a good-quality range of cycle wear that is also fashionable.

Student .... would not be awarded full marks because ....

....

....

....

....

....

....

....

....

I use a highlighter when reading the question, to underline the business term and also the reference to the extract. For example, in the question above I would highlight 'market segment' as the business term and 'brand of cycle wear' as the reference to the extract. This helps me to make sure I am answering the precise question.

Hint
Always look at the number of marks available for a question. This gives a good indication of how much development is needed in the answer.

Complete the answer

1 Complete the student's answer so it would be awarded 6 marks.

4 (b) Brad is keen to build his brand Moser using digital communication. Analyse the benefit to Brad of using digital communication.

(6)

> **Hint**
> One benefit has been identified. The question asks you to 'analyse' the benefit, so now you need to develop the answer. The command word analyse requires detailed interconnected points.

Nearly there

One benefit of using digital communication is that social media is popular with young people. This will allow Brad to promote his brand with images of cyclists wearing his goods. This will be shared by followers, allowing it to reach a wider target market.

....

....

....

....

....

....

....

> When given additional information at the start of a question, I always try to include this in my answer. It helps me to plan where my answer is going to end.

Connect the comments

1 Draw lines to connect the marker's comments to the relevant parts of the student's answer. One has been done for you. Some comments may relate to more than one sentence in the student's answer.

4   (b) Analyse the benefit to Brad of using primary market research.   (6)

> **Hint**
> When answering a 6-mark question you can choose one of two approaches: EITHER write one relevant point with five connected strands (one long paragraph), OR two relevant points each with two to three strands (two shorter paragraphs). Either way there must be five linked strands across your answer.

Had a go

Brad could use focus groups to find out what

cyclists want in branded cycle wear.

This would allow him to collect information about

preferences such as colours and styles.

He could then use this information to help

develop his clothes. This would mean that they

meet the needs and wants of the customer.

However, this could be time consuming and cost

money, which would mean that Brad could not

launch his new clothes onto the market quickly.

There are a number of developed points as to how Brad could make use of this information to help him design his clothes.

The student makes good use of the context, explaining how a focus group could be used to find out about a range of cycle wear.

The student moves away from answering the question by talking about a disadvantage rather than staying focused on the benefit.

A correct benefit has been identified showing accurate knowledge. This clearly shows an understanding of primary market research.

Underline or highlight what you have been asked to analyse and stay focused on this word. Here, I would have highlighted the word 'benefit' to make sure I was only talking about the benefits.

Mark the answer

1 Use the mark scheme below to assign a mark to the student's answer on page 19. Explain your decision.

Level	Mark	Descriptor
	0	No rewardable material.
Level 1	1–2	• Limited application of knowledge and understanding of business concepts and issues to the business context (AO2). • Attempts to deconstruct business information and/or issues, finding limited connections between points (AO3a).
Level 2	3–4	• Sound application of knowledge and understanding of business concepts and issues to the business context, although there may be some inconsistencies (AO2). • Deconstructs business information and/or issues, finding interconnected points with chain of reasoning, although there may be some logical inconsistencies (AO3a).
Level 3	5–6	• Detailed application of knowledge and understanding of business concepts and issues to the business context throughout (AO2). • Deconstructs business information and/or issues, finding detailed interconnected points with logical chains of reasoning (AO3a).

I would award the student's answer .... out of 6 marks because ....

....

....

....

....

....

....

....

....

....

....

Find the answer

1 Which **one** of the student's answers below would be awarded 2 marks?

Brad has forecast the following sales and costs for the first 3 months of 2019.

	January	February	March
Sales revenue	£5000	£5500	£7500
Total costs	£4000	£4200	£5000
Profit	£1000	£1300	£2500

Table 3

5 (b) Using the information in **Table 3**, calculate the average profit. You are advised to show your workings. **(2)**

A   £5000 + £5500 + £7500 = £18000 $\dfrac{£18\,000}{3} = £6000$

B   £1060

C   £5000 + £4000 + £1000 = £10000 $\dfrac{£10\,000}{3} = £3333.33$

D   £1000 + £1300 + £2500 = £4800 $\dfrac{£4800}{3} = £1600$

E   £5000 + £5500 + £7500 × 3 = £54000 $\dfrac{£54\,000}{3} = £18\,000$

F   £1000 + £1300 + £2500 = £4800 $\dfrac{£4800}{3} = £2000$

> **Hint**
> Always show your workings. Student B may have just written their answer down incorrectly and would be awarded 0 marks. If they had shown their workings, they may still have got 1 mark, even though their answer was incorrect.

Answer .... would get 2 marks because ....

....

....

....

> I always check my answer by doing the calculation twice. It is easy to press the wrong number when using a calculator, so by checking that I get the same answer twice, I can be confident that I haven't made a mistake!

Complete the question

1 There are several parts missing from this question. Use the student answers to complete the questions.

Brad has forecast the following sales and costs for the first three months of 2021.

His selling price per unit is . . . .

	January	February	March
Fixed costs	£1600	£	£ . . . .
Variable costs per unit	£15	£15	£15
Number of units sold	200	220	300
Sales	£5000	£5500	£7500
Profit	£400	£600	£1400

Table 4

5 (a) Calculate Brad's . . . . for March.

You are advised to show your . . . .

(2)

Nailed it!

$$\frac{\text{Fixed costs}}{(\text{selling price} - \text{variable costs})} = \frac{£1600}{(£25 - £15)} = \frac{£1600}{£10} = 160 \text{ units}$$

(b) Calculate Brad's . . . . for . . . .
your workings.

(2)

Nailed it!

Number of units sold – break-even level of output . . . .

= 200 – 160 . . . .

= 40 units . . . .

> **Hint**
> In the exam you might need to be able to rearrange a formula to identify a missing figure. It is a good idea to practise doing this.

When revising I wrote all of the formulas out on one piece of A3 paper. I then made sure at least once a week I looked at the formula to try and memorise them. Each week it got easier to remember all of the formulas.

Complete the answer

1 Complete the student answers below so that each one would gain the maximum of 2 marks.

Brad has forecast the following sales and costs for the second three months of 2019. His selling price per unit has gone up to £30.

	April	May	June
Fixed costs	£1600	£1600	£1600
Variable costs per unit	£17.20	£17.20	£17.20
Number of units sold	300	350	480

Table 5

5 (a) Calculate Brad's break-even level of output for May. You are advised to show your workings. (2)

Nearly there

$$\frac{\text{Fixed costs}}{(\text{selling price} - \text{variable costs})}$$

(b) Calculate Brad's sales revenue for May. You are advised to show your workings. (2)

Had a go

350 × £17.20 = £6020

....

....

....

....

Hint
Always show your working out. This will help you to gain marks even if your answer is incorrect. It will prove that you have understood the process.

Find the answer

1 A student has written three paragraphs in response to the question below. Which **two** paragraphs would you include in your answer? Explain your choice. Then explain why you would **not** include the other paragraph.

5 (c) Analyse the impact on Brad of changes in technology. **(6)**

Paragraph A

> One impact for Brad is he will be able to reach a wider target market to sell his cycle wear. This is because he can reach a national and international market through social media, for example by posting pictures of his branded clothing on Instagram. Therefore, the reputation of his brand will be widespread among cyclists. This will allow him to increase sales. This means that he will be able to reach his break-even point and start to make a profit.

Paragraph B

> Changes in technology can have a negative impact on Brad because there will be increased competition. This is because his costs will be lower as he does not have an expensive shop to run. Therefore, he will be able to sell his cycle wear cheaply gaining a good reputation among cyclists who want quality and fashion. This will allow Brad to expand his business by designing new ranges.

Paragraph C

> One negative impact on Brad is that his brand reputation could be damaged by poor reviews on social media. This is because sites such as Facebook allow customers to write comments and blogs. Therefore, if Brad was to supply poor-quality cycle wear to cyclists, they may give him a poor rating. This could be quickly spread among followers who subscribe to speciality interest pages for cyclists. Therefore, Brad would have to invest in promoting his brand more to try and rebuild its reputation, which would increase his costs.

> **Hint**
> Think carefully about the options you have chosen. What is the opposite outcome of your decision?

I would include paragraphs ...... and ...... because ....

....

....

....

I would not include paragraph ...... because ....

....

....

Complete the answer

1 Complete the student's answer so it would be awarded 6 marks.

5 (c) Analyse the impact on Brad of changes in technology. **(6)**

> **Hint**
> For each point made, you need to develop a logical chain of reasoning in context.
> Make sure you use connectives, such as 'this means', 'therefore' and 'leading to', to show
> your linked points.

Had a go

Changes in technology can have a negative impact on Brad because there will be increased

competition. This is because it will be easy for other new businesses to set up an

e-commerce site selling cycle wear.

....

....

....

A second impact is an increase in brand awareness through social

media sites.

....

....

....

....

....

....

....

> **Hint**
> To make sure your answer is in context, use words and phrases from the case study
> throughout your answer. For example, for this question, your might refer to 'cycle wear',
> 'amateur cyclists' and 'positive reviews on social media'.

Mark the answer

1 Read the six student answers shown below.

(a) Which three would you award 1 mark to? Explain your answer.

(b) Which three would you not award a mark to? Explain your answer.

6 (a) State **one** impact on Brad of increased competition.   (1)

Question	Answer	Mark
6 (a)	Award 1 mark for stating one impact on Brad of increased competition. Do not award marks for impacts that would not be appropriate for Brad.	1

A   Brad would see a fall in sales.

B   Lower revenue from selling branded cycle wear.

C   Lower profits, as customers will go elsewhere.

D   Brad would need to keep his shop open for longer to attract customers.

E   Brad would need to dedicate more time to promoting the brand on social media.

F   Need to improve customer service by ensuring online orders are posted quickly.

(a) ...I would award 1 mark to ......,...... and ...... because ....
....
....
....

(b) ...I would not award a mark to ......,...... and ...... because ....
....
....
....
....

> **Hint**
> Remember, using the name of the character in the case study does not make your answer applicable. It has to be something specific to that business.

Mark the answer

1 Complete the student's answer so it would be awarded 2 marks.

6 (b) Outline **one** way that Brad meets customer needs. (2)

> **Hint**
> One way has been identified. The question asks you to 'outline' one way, so now you need to develop the answer to explain the stated method. You only need one step in your development.

Nearly there

He provides customers with a choice of goods. ....

....

....

....

....

2 Complete the student's answer so it would be awarded 2 marks.

6 (b) Outline **one** way that Brad meets customer needs. (2)

> **Hint**
> This time the supporting explanation has been identified, so you now need to identify the method being explained.

Nearly there

....

....

Meaning that his customers will be satisfied that their cycle wear will be durable. ....

> I always try to leave time at the end of an exam to go back and check what I have written. Sometimes I find a silly mistake or realise I need to add another sentence to develop my explanation.

Connect the comments

1 Draw lines to connect the marker's comments to the relevant parts of the student's answer. One has been done for you. Some comments may relate to more than one sentence in the student's answer.

> **Hint**
> This is just the first paragraph of the student's answer; it is not the whole answer.

Brad is considering two options to expand his business:
Option 1: Add a range of running wear to his products.
Option 2: Open a store near the university.

6 (c) Justify which **one** of these two options Brad should choose.   (9)

Had a go

Brad should choose option 2 to open a new store.

This is because it will raise the profile of the business.

Being close to the university will mean that a lot of

students will see his shop and go in. They will then want

to buy his clothes because they are of good quality

and reasonably priced. This means they will appeal

to students as a target market. Sales will therefore

increase. As more students see others wearing the

cycle wear and also see the shop, awareness of the

brand will grow further, leading to an increase in revenue.

....

....

The student starts their answer with a clear judgement that option 2 should be chosen.

The paragraph is then developed with a number of interconnected points showing a logical chain of reasoning.

The judgement is then backed with a relevant argument.

The student's argument is placed in context by considering the location of the store.

> When planning my answers to the 9-mark 'Justify' questions, I go back to the case study and see whether I can find arguments for and against both options. I then decide which option I think is best before starting to write my answer. I can then tell the examiner what option I am going for in my opening sentence.

Find the answer

1 A student has written three paragraphs in response to the question on page 28. Their first paragraph is shown on page 28. One of the paragraphs below is to be the second paragraph in their answer.

(a) Which paragraph would you include as the second paragraph in the student's answer? Explain your choice.

(b) Then explain why you would **not** include the other two paragraphs.

Paragraph A

I wouldn't choose option 1 because Brad is a keen cyclist and building a brand for cycle wear. He is unlikely to know about running and might therefore design running gear that is not popular or fashionable because he does not understand the market. So he would waste a lot of money on research and development for a product that may not sell. Whereas we know he knows about cycle wear and has done market research, plus his brand is already known and liked by many cyclists.

Paragraph B

Another reason to open a shop near the university is because the land is likely to be cheaper than in a city centre. Therefore, he would be close to the market but with lower costs. This would help Brad to break even in the store quicker, as his fixed costs will be lower. He will therefore have a higher margin of safety. This means he will be able to make a profit based on a large number of students visiting his store and shopping there.

Paragraph C

However, opening a store will prove expensive. While operating via his website, Brad does not have high overhead costs such as rent and heating and lighting. A store would increase his fixed costs making it more difficult for Brad to make a profit. This is especially true as he may not make enough sales to cover costs. Students, who do not have a lot of money, may not want to buy cycle wear but rather make do with their everyday clothes. This may lead to Brad having cash flow problems as the cash coming in from sales may not be enough to cover his monthly cash outflows for rent and bills. This could lead to failure for Brad.

(a) I would include paragraph .... because ....

....

....

(b) I would not include paragraphs .... and .... because ....

....

....

....

Mark the answer

Read the first two paragraphs of the student's answer on pages 28 and 29. Then read the student's final paragraph below, which is their conclusion to the question on page 28.

Use the mark scheme below to decide what mark you would give the student's answer as a whole. Justify your decision.

In conclusion, Brad should open a new store near the university because this will allow him to attract a large number of students into his store. They will be attracted by his reasonable prices and high quality, meaning his revenues will be high enough to cover his additional costs. However, this will depend upon him being able to find premises that are in a good location but not too expensive.

Level	Mark	Descriptor
	0	No rewardable material.
Level 1	1–3	• Limited application of knowledge and understanding of business concepts and issues to the business context (AO2). • Attempts to deconstruct business information and/or issues, finding limited connections between points (AO3a). • Makes a judgement, providing a simple justification based on limited evaluation of business information and issues relevant to the choice made (AO3b).
Level 2	4–6	• Sound application of knowledge and understanding of business concepts and issues to the business context, although there may be some inconsistencies (AO2). • Deconstructs business information and/or issues, finding interconnected points with chain of reasoning, although there may be some logical inconsistencies (AO3a). • Makes a judgement, providing a justification based on sound evaluation of business information and issues relevant to the choice made (AO3b).
Level 3	7–9	• Detailed application of knowledge and understanding of business concepts and issues to the business context throughout (AO2). • Deconstructs business information and/or issues, finding detailed interconnected points with logical chains of reasoning (AO3a). • Makes a judgement, providing a clear justification based on a thorough evaluation of business information and issues relevant to the choice made (AO3b).

I would give the student's answer ..... out of 9 marks because ....

....

....

....

....

....

....

....

....

....

Case study

Jock and Patricia met when working at a bakery in York, where they worked alongside the head chef to create magnificent cakes and pastries. Soon they realised their real passion was chocolate. In 2016 they left the restaurant and set up a small chocolatier, Mr Nibs. The entrepreneurs set a social objective to only source the finest cocoa from the Ivory Coast and to ensure farmers were paid a fair rate and were well looked after.

At first all the chocolates were made by Jock and Patricia in Jock's kitchen and sold at food markets. As they became more successful, they struggled to cope with demand and decided to invest in a small commercial kitchen. This would allow them to increase output and sell their chocolates online with delivery across the UK, as well as continuing to have stalls at food markets. Jock and Patricia plan to still make all the chocolates themselves and be the two people attending all the food markets.

Buying the kitchen and equipment would cost £750000. They decided to raise this finance through a bank loan. The loan would be secured against Jock's house so if they default on payments the bank could take his home away.

Mr Nibs operates in a very competitive market. York alone has more than 10 independent chocolatiers. Then there are the big businesses operating in the market, such as Nestlé, Mars and Ferrero. However, Jock and Patricia are confident that there is sufficient demand to continue to grow. They have used market research to identify trends in the market.

> **Hint**
> Underline or highlight the key information in the extract.

Find the answer

1 Find the answer that would be awarded 1 mark. Choose **A**, **B** or **C**. Explain your choice.

7   (a)   State **one** stakeholder of Mr Nibs.   **(1)**

Question	Answer	Mark
7 (a)	Award 1 mark for stating one stakeholder of Mr Nibs. Do not accept stakeholders that do not apply to Mr Nibs.	1

A   Shareholders

B   Suppliers

C   Employees

> **Hint**
> Read the question carefully and consider the context of the case study. Shareholders, suppliers and employees are all types of stakeholders, but which one is relevant to Mr Nibs?

Answer .... would be awarded 1 mark because ....

....

2 Find the answer that would be awarded 1 mark. Choose **A**, **B** or **C**. Explain your choice.

7   (a)   State **one** type of ownership suitable to Mr Nibs.   **(1)**

Question	Answer	Mark
7 (a)	Award 1 mark for stating one type of ownership suitable to Mr Nibs. Do not accept types of ownership that are not suitable to Mr Nibs.	1

A   Sole trader

B   Private limited company

C   Franchising

Answer .... would be awarded 1 mark because ....

....

....

....

> When the command word is 'state', I try to answer the question in less than seven words. There is no need to write in complete sentences. This saves me time so that I do not run out of time on the higher mark questions.

Complete the answer

1 Complete the student's answer so it would be awarded 2 marks.

Figure 2 shows the actual and forecast value of the chocolate market in £ millions.

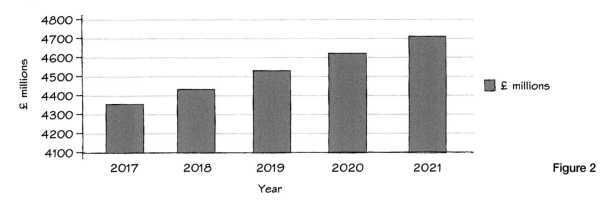

Figure 2

> **Hint**
> Remember that the information presented in graphs will be stated on each axis. It is important to read the axis carefully.

7   (b)   Using **Figure 2**, calculate the forecast growth in the chocolate market from 2020 to 2021.   **(2)**

2020 = 4620

2021 = 4710

....

....

2 Complete the student's answer so it would be awarded 2 marks.

7   (b)   Using **Figure 2**, calculate the forecast growth in the chocolate market from 2017 to 2021.   **(2)**

2017 = 4360

2021 = 4710

....

....

> **Hint**
> Always show your working out. This will help you to improve the quality of your response even if your answer is incorrect. It will prove that you have understood the process.

Complete the question

1 Complete the question by filling in the missing word or words.

> 7   (a)   State **one** .... that Mr Nibs would have to pay.   **(1)**
>
> Nailed it!
>
> Cocoa beans ....

2 Complete the question by filling in the missing word or words.

> 7   (a)   State **one** .... that Mr Nibs would have to pay.   **(1)**
>
> Nailed it!
>
> Rent on the kitchen ....

3 Complete the question by filling in the missing word or words.

> 7   (a)   State **one** .... that Mr Nibs would show on the cash flow forecast.   **(1)**
>
> Nailed it!
>
> Money from customers at food markets ....

4 Complete the question by filling in the missing word or words.

> 7   (a)   State **one** .... need that Mr Nibs' customers would have.   **(1)**
>
> Nailed it!
>
> Choice of flavours ....

5 Complete the question by filling in the missing word or words.

> 7   (a)   State **one** .... of Mr Nibs.   **(1)**
>
> Nailed it!
>
> Other chocolatiers in York ....

When I was revising, I made my own glossary of key terms to help remember what each term meant.

When answering 1-mark questions, I try to ensure my answer is specific to the business and the products in the extract.

Build the answer

1 Look at the question below and the list of ideas the student has extracted from the case study on page 31. The student has decided to choose option 2.

Which ideas (items A–J) would you use in a plan to answer this question? Tick the top five pieces of information you would use.

To increase profits Jock and Patricia are considering two options:

Option 1: Buying cheaper ingredients from different suppliers.

Option 2: Employing an assistant to attend food markets and maintain the website.

7 (d) Justify which **one** of these two options Mr Nibs should choose. **(9)**

> **Hint**
> Read through items A–J carefully before making your selection.

A	Their real passion was chocolate	☐
B	Set a social objective to only source the finest cocoa from the Ivory Coast	☐
C	To ensure farmers are paid a fair rate and well looked after	☐
D	Invest in a small commercial kitchen	☐
E	Still make all the chocolate themselves	☐
F	The two people attending all the food markets	☐
G	Buying the kitchen and equipment would cost £750 000	☐
H	Operates in a very competitive market	☐
I	There are big businesses operating in the market	☐
J	Confident that there is sufficient demand to continue to grow	☐

2 Look at the five items you have ticked. Choose **one** you would use in your argument **for** option 2. Justify your choice.

> **Suggested answer**

....

....

....

....

Mark the answer

1 Use the mark scheme below to decide how many marks you would award the student's answer. Justify your decision.

To increase profits Jock and Patricia are considering two options:

Option 1: Buying cheaper ingredients from different suppliers.

Option 2: Employing an assistant to attend food markets and maintain the website.

7 (d) Justify which **one** of these two options Mr Nibs should choose. (9)

Jock and Patricia should choose option 1. By changing to a cheaper supplier for raw materials, such as cocoa, variable costs will go down. This will allow them to lower the price charged to customers. This is important because they operate in a competitive market with 10 independent chocolatiers in York. Therefore, they will attract more customers increasing profit. However, this could damage the reputation of the brand. This is because they are no longer meeting the social objective of paying a fair rate to farmers.

Overall option 1 is the best because they do everything themselves and therefore shouldn't employ an assistant. This is a bad idea as it would raise costs and therefore lower profit.

Level	Mark	Descriptor
	0	No rewardable material.
Level 1	1–3	• Limited application of knowledge and understanding of business concepts and issues to the business context (AO2). • Attempts to deconstruct business information and/or issues, finding limited connections between points (AO3a). • Makes a judgement, providing a simple justification based on limited evaluation of business information and issues relevant to the choice made (AO3b).
Level 2	4–6	• Sound application of knowledge and understanding of business concepts and issues to the business context, although there may be some inconsistencies (AO2). • Deconstructs business information and/or issues, finding interconnected points with chain of reasoning, although there may be some logical inconsistencies (AO3a). • Makes a judgement, providing a justification based on sound evaluation of business information and issues relevant to the choice made (AO3b).
Level 3	7–9	• Detailed application of knowledge and understanding of business concepts and issues to the business context throughout (AO2). • Deconstructs business information and/or issues, finding detailed interconnected points with logical chains of reasoning (AO3a). • Makes a judgement, providing a clear justification based on a thorough evaluation of business information and issues relevant to the choice made (AO3b).

I would award the student's answer .... out of 9 marks because ....

Suggested answer

....

....

....

Connect the comments

1 Draw lines to connect the marker's comments to the relevant parts of the student's answer. One has been done for you. Some comments may relate to more than one sentence in the student's answer.

> **Hint**
> This is just the first paragraph of the student's answer – it is not the whole answer.

7 (e) Evaluate whether a loan was a good source of finance for Mr Nibs. You should use the information provided as well as your knowledge of business. **(12)**

> Nailed it!

Jock and Patricia were right to use a loan from the bank. This is because it would mean they received the whole £750 000 in one payment from the bank. Therefore, they would be able to buy and equip their kitchen quickly. This is important because it would allow them to increase their supply of chocolate, which they needed to do to match demand, as they were struggling in Jock's kitchen. This would therefore allow them to sell more and increase revenue. This is important for all small businesses that are looking to grow. Mr Nibs should take advantage of this, especially as their cocoa is fair trade and society is increasingly concerned about shopping ethically.

The student shows that they understand what a loan is.

The student's answer starts with a clear statement telling the examiner that this paragraph is going to look at why a loan was the right choice.

The argument is placed in context by considering why Jock and Patricia need a loan.

The paragraph is then developed with a number of interconnected points showing a logical chain of reasoning.

The student successfully brings in their own knowledge of business to support their argument.

There is a further reference to the case study.

> The more I understood what examiners are looking for when answering the different types of questions, the better my answers became.

Build the answer

1 Complete paragraphs 2 and 3 of the student's answer to the question on page 37. First, re-read the student's first paragraph on page 37. You will also need to re-read the case study on page 31.

> **Hint**
> Remember, you need a number of interconnected points in context. You should also aim to bring something from the real world into your answer.

Had a go

However, a bank loan may not have been a good source of finance. This is because ....

....

....

....

....

....

....

....

....

....

....

....

Overall, I think that a bank loan was a good idea for Jock and Patricia because ....

....

....

....

....

....

....

....

> **Hint**
> Remember, your answer to the 12-mark 'Evaluate' questions must show balance. You can achieve this by discussing the advantages of both options or the advantage and disadvantage of just one option.

> **Hint**
> In your answer to a 12-mark 'Evaluate' question, aim to use the 'it depends' rule in your final paragraph. After saying which option the business should choose and why, the final sentence should consider a factor that the success of this option depends on.

Find the answer

1 Find the answer that would be awarded 1 mark. Choose **A**, **B**, **C** or **D**. Explain your choice.

> **Hint**
> Some questions must be answered with a tick in a box. If you change your mind about an answer, put a line through the box and then mark your new answer with a tick.

1 (a) Which **one** of the following is an example of internal growth?

Select **one** answer. **(1)**

☐ **A** Merger

☐ **B** New products

☐ **C** Inorganic growth

☐ **D** Takeover

Answer .... would be awarded 1 mark because ....

....

....

....

2 Find the student's answer that would be awarded 1 mark. Choose **A**, **B**, **C** or **D**.
Explain your choice.

1 (b) Which **one** of the following is a non-financial method of motivating an employee?

Select **one** answer. **(1)**

☐ **A** Promotion

☐ **B** Fringe benefits

☐ **C** Job enrichment

☐ **D** Remuneration

Answer .... would be awarded 1 mark because ....

....

....

....

> When answering multiple choice questions, I always underline or highlight the key business term in the question. This helps me to focus. Here I would have focused on non-financial motivator.

Complete the question

1 Complete the question by adding three multiple choice options. Make sure only one is correct.

1   (a)   Which **one** of the following methods of promotion makes use of technology?
Select **one** answer.   (1)

☑ **A** ....

☐ **B** ....

☐ **C** Product trials

☐ **D** ....

> I always have a copy of the specification on my desk when I am revising.
> This helps me know what business terms come under each topic.

2 Complete the question by adding four multiple choice options. Make sure only one is correct.

1   (b)   Which **one** of the following is a barrier to international trade?
Select **one** answer.   (1)

☐ **A** ....

☐ **B** ....

☐ **C** ....

☑ **D** ....

Improve the answer

1 Use the hints below to write an improved answer to this question.

1 (c) Explain **one** benefit to a growing business of globalisation. (3)

> **Hint**
> Remember, for 3-mark 'Explain' questions there is 1 mark for stating a correct point, in this case a benefit. The further 2 marks are for explaining the benefit.

Had a go

Opportunity to sell overseas.

> **Hint**
> For this style of question, you need to make a relevant point followed by two strands in a line of argument. Use connectives such as 'this means that', 'therefore' and 'leading to' to help you develop your answer.

2 Use the hints below to write an improved answer to this question.

1 (d) Explain **one** drawback to a business of using job production. (3)

Nearly there

One drawback is that the rate at which goods are produced is likely to be slower.

This is because each item is made individually to meet the needs of the customer.

Complete the answer

1 Complete the student's answer so it would be awarded 3 marks.

1 (c) Explain **one** drawback to a business of using loan capital as a source of finance. **(3)**

> **Hint**
> One drawback has been identified. The question asks you to 'explain' one drawback, so now you need to develop the answer to explain the disadvantage. Try to use two steps in your development.

Nearly there

One drawback is that the bank will charge interest. ....

....

....

....

....

....

2 Complete the student's answer so it would be awarded 3 marks.

1 (d) Explain **one** impact of technology on human resources. **(3)**

> **Hint**
> This time the supporting explanation has been identified, so you now need to identify the impact being explained.

Nearly there

....

This will give them greater flexibility to work hours that suit from their own homes. As ....

a result, employee motivation is likely to be higher. ....

....

....

....

I try to make sure that I use a business term in each sentence, so that my answers demonstrate my knowledge of the subject.

Mark the answer

1 A student has written an answer to this question. Use the marking instructions below to decide how many marks you would award the student's answer.

---

1 (c) Explain **one** benefit of a motivated workforce. (3)

One benefit is retaining employees. This means that they will stay with the business for

longer. Therefore, recruitment costs will be lower.

Question	Answer	Mark
1 (c)	Award 1 mark for identification of a benefit, plus 2 further marks for explaining this benefit up to a total of 3 marks. Answers that list more than one benefit with no explanation will be awarded a maximum of 1 mark.	3

I would award the student's answer out of 3 marks because

....

....

....

....

....

....

....

....

....

....

I practised writing under timed conditions. This really helped in the exam, as I remained focused and didn't write too much on short-answer questions. This meant I could answer all the questions in the time allowed.

Complete the question

1 Complete the question by adding three multiple choice options. Make sure two are correct.

> **Hint**
> Multiple choice questions often have answers that are believable but incorrect. These are called distractors. Try to make it relatively difficult to spot the incorrect answer.

2 (a) Which **two** of the following are phases in the product life cycle?

Select **two** answers. **(2)**

- [ ] **A** Market research
- [ ] **B** ....
- [✓] **C** ....
- [✓] **D** ....
- [ ] **E** Market segmentation

2 Complete the question by adding three multiple choice options. Make sure two are correct.

2 (b) Which **two** of the following are benefits to a business of centralised decision-making?

Select **two** answers. **(2)**

- [✓] **A** ....
- [✓] **B** ....
- [ ] **C** ....
- [ ] **D** Decisions shared with branches
- [ ] **E** Decision-makers may know their customers better

> My teacher gave me a copy of the specification for GCSE Business at the beginning of Year 10. It is a useful document to see what you need to know and it really helps me with revision.

Mark the answer

1 Find the answers that would be awarded 2 marks. Choose two answers from **A, B, C, D** and **E**. Explain your choice.

> **Hint**
> Some questions must be answered with a tick in a box. If you change your mind about an answer, put a line through the box and then mark your new answer with a tick.

2 (a) Which **two** of the following are stages in the sales process?
Select **two** answers. **(2)**

☐ **A** Taking money

☐ **B** Quality control

☐ **C** Responses to customer feedback

☐ **D** Relationship with suppliers

☐ **E** Product knowledge

Answers ...... and ...... would be awarded 1 mark each because ....

....

....

....

2 Find the answer that would be awarded 2 marks. Choose two answers from **A, B, C, D** and **E**. Explain your choice.

2 (b) Which **two** of the following are documents used in the recruitment process?
Select **two** answers. **(2)**

☐ **A** Interviews

☐ **B** Person specification

☐ **C** Birth certificate

☐ **D** Application form

☐ **E** Attracting employees

> When revising processes or lists, I often draw them as a flow chart or spider diagram. This helps me to remember them, which means I feel more confident when answering multiple choice questions.

Answers ...... and ...... would be awarded 1 mark each because ....

....

....

....

Find the answer

1 Find the student's answer that would be awarded 2 marks. Explain your choice.

Table 1 contains information about a business.

Cost of sales	£250 000
Sales revenue	£480 000
Other expenses	£120 000

Table 1

2 (c) Using the information in Table 1, calculate the gross profit for the business. You are advised to show your workings.

(2)

A £480 000 + £250 000 = £730 000

B £480 000 − £250 000 − £120 000 = £110 000

C $\dfrac{£230\,000}{£480\,000} \times 100 = 48\%$

D £250 000 − £480 000 = (£230 000)

E $\dfrac{£480\,000}{£250\,000} \times 100 = 19\%$

F £480 000 − £250 000 = £230 000

G £480 000 + £250 000 − £120 000 = £610 000

Answer .... would get 2 marks because ....

....

....

....

....

Hint

Always show your workings. If you make a mistake but the examiner can see you were on the right track, you may still be awarded a mark.

Complete the answer

1 Complete the student's answer below so that it would be awarded 2 marks.

Table 2 contains information about a business.

Gross profit	£980 000
Sales revenue	£2 500 000
Net profit	£520 000

Table 2

2 (c) Using the information in **Table 2**, calculate the gross profit margin for the business. You are advised to show your workings. **(2)**

> **Hint**
> In calculation questions, unless given specific instructions, it is a good idea to round a percentage up to a whole number.

Nearly there

$$\frac{£980\,000}{£2\,500\,000}$$

2 Complete the student's answer below so that it would be awarded 2 marks.

2 (c) Using the information in **Table 2** above, calculate the net profit margin for the business. You are advised to show your workings. **(2)**

Had a go

$$\frac{£520\,000}{} \times 100$$

Complete the question

1 Complete the question by filling in the missing words.

> **2** (d) Explain **one** .... to a business of making a .... decision. **(3)**
>
> (Nailed it!)
>
> Raw materials will be of the correct quality. Therefore, the business can produce a ....
>
> quality product. This will allow it to meet the needs of the customer. ....
>
> ....
>
> ....
>
> ....

2 Complete the question by filling in the missing words.

> **2** (d) Explain **one** .... to a business of .... **(3)**
>
> (Nailed it!)
>
> There may be a lack of new ideas brought into the business. This would mean that new ....
>
> processes are not introduced. This could lead to a loss of competitive advantage in ....
>
> the future. ....
>
> ....
>
> ....

I always underline the key parts of the question before starting my answer.
For example, for the 3-mark 'Explain' questions, I always check whether the
question is asking for an advantage, disadvantage, impact or drawback.

Odd one out

1 Use the mark scheme below to decide which of these student answers would **not** be awarded 3 marks. Explain your decision.

2 (e) Explain **one** reason why a business might use market data to inform business decisions. **(3)**

> **Hint**
> Always read the question very carefully. Sometimes there are terms that are easy to confuse, such as 'market data' and 'marketing data'.

Question	Answer	Mark
2 (e)	Award 1 mark for identification of a reason, plus 2 further marks for explaining the reason up to a total of 3 marks.	3

A   Market data will provide information about demographics. Therefore, the business will be able to identify a suitable target market. This will allow it to design goods to meet the needs of customers.

B   One reason is to collect information on levels of customer satisfaction. This will allow a business to identify any weaknesses in its service. It can therefore make improvements to help build its reputation.

C   Market data will indicate the size of the market to a business. This will allow it to better forecast sales. This means it will be able to plan how much of a product to produce to meet demand.

D   One reason would be to identify the number of competitors. This would help indicate where there is opportunity for growth. This would help inform future plans for new outlets.

Answer .... would **not** be awarded full marks because ....

....

....

....

....

....

....

....

....

> I use a highlighter when reading the question to underline the business term. This helps me to make sure I am answering the precise question asked.

Find the answer

1 Find the answer that would be awarded 1 mark. Choose **A, B, C** or **D**. Explain your choice.

> **Hint**
> When answering a multiple choice question, it is important to read all of the options carefully. The examiner will often include an answer that is quite close to the correct one.
> If you cross through the answers you know are wrong first, this will help you to narrow down the correct answer.

3 (a) Which **one** of the following is an advantage of motivation?
Select **one** answer.
(1)

☐ **A** Internal recruitment

☐ **B** Productivity

☐ **C** Flow production

☐ **D** Decentralisation

Answer .... would be awarded 1 mark because ....

....

....

....

2 Find the answer that would be awarded 1 mark. Choose **A, B, C** or **D**. Explain your choice.

3 (a) Which **one** of the following is an example of financial data that can be used to justify business decisions?
Select **one** answer.
(1)

☐ **A** Customer opinions

☐ **B** Growth of market

> When answering multiple choice questions, I always read all of the answers before making my decision about which one is correct.

☐ **C** Sales revenue

☐ **D** Demographics

Answer .... would be awarded 1 mark because ....

....

....

....

Complete the question

1 Complete the question by filling in the missing words.

Table 3 contains information about a new machine that the business will keep for .... years.

Total profit	....
.... of new machine	£80 000

Table 3

3 (b) Using the information in **Table 3**, calculate the .... rate of return for the new machine.

You are advised to ....

(2)

Nailed it!

$$\frac{£450\,000}{3} = £150\,000$$

$$\frac{£150\,000}{£80\,000} \times 100 = 188\%$$

Hint
In calculation questions, unless given specific instructions, it is a good idea to round a percentage up to a whole number.

2 Complete the question by filling in the missing words.

Table 4 contains information about a business.

.... of sales	....
Sales	....
.... profit	£84 000

Table 4

3 (b) Using the information in **Table 4**, calculate the ....

You are advised to ....

(2)

Nailed it!

£650 000 − £400 000 = £250 000

Complete the answer

1 Complete the student's answer so it would be awarded 3 marks.

3   (c)   Explain **one** benefit to a business of training employees.   **(3)**

> **Hint**
> One benefit has been identified. The question asks you to 'explain' one benefit, so now you need to develop the answer to explain the benefit. Try to use two steps in your development.

Nearly there

One benefit is that employees will have the necessary skills.

....

....

....

....

2 Complete the student's answer so it would be awarded 3 marks.

3   (d)   Explain **one** benefit to a business of using technology in production.   **(3)**

> **Hint**
> This time the supporting explanation has been identified, so you now need to identify the impact being explained.

Nearly there

....

This will allow the business to alter the number and types of goods produced.

Doing this means the business will be better able to respond to customer needs.

....

....

> I try to make sure that my first point uses the wording of the specification, so that the examiner knows I have understood all the topics.

Mark the answer

1 A student has written an answer to this question. Use the marking instructions below to decide how many marks you would award the answer.

---

3 (c) Explain **one** impact of quality assurance. **(3)**

One impact is that the business will have to employ a specialist to check the quality of a product once it has been made. This means that if there is a fault it will only be picked up once the product is finished. This could lead to a large wastage cost.

Question	Answer	Mark
3 (c)	Award 1 mark for identification of an impact, plus 2 further marks for explaining this impact, up to a total of 3 marks. Answers that list more than one impact with no explanation will be awarded a maximum of 1 mark.	3

I would award this student's answer .... out of 3 marks because ....

....

....

> In my notes I highlighted terms that were easily confused. This prompted me to consider the term in the question carefully before writing my answers. This helped me to avoid answering a question based on an incorrect starting point.

---

2 A student has written an answer to the following question. Choose which of the marker's comments it would be appropriate to use as feedback to the student.

---

3 (d) Explain **one** disadvantage to a business of behaving ethically. **(3)**

Nailed it!

One disadvantage is that costs to the business may be higher. This means that there will be a trade-off with profit. Therefore, the business may not be able to fund future growth.

A Well done, you have identified three relevant points to gain all 3 marks. ☐

B Good use of business terminology; however, I would like to see more strands to your argument. ☐

C One disadvantage identified and clearly explained with two strands in your development. ☐

D Good work, there are three clear strands in your answer. ☐

Re-order the answer

1 The sentences below are taken from a paragraph written by a student in response to the
following question. Rearrange the sentences into the most logical order by numbering
them 1 to 6.

3 (e) Discuss the benefit to a business of being ethical. (6)

> **Hint**
> It's important that answers to this type of question are in a logical order. Make sure you
> read your answer through from the start to check it makes sense.

Nailed it!

.... This will lead to repeat custom. ....

....

.... Consequently, the business will enjoy high sales while keeping its costs low. ....

....

.... One benefit is that stakeholders will recognise that the business is behaving in a way .....

.... that people generally consider to be good. ....

....

.... This will allow the business to enjoy higher net profit margins. ....

....

.... Therefore, the business will gain a reputation for treating stakeholders well. ....

....

.... As a result, the business will need to spend less on advertising. ....

....

When writing a longer response, I try to use a variety of phrases to help me build
a developed argument, such as 'therefore', 'as a result', 'meaning that', etc.

Connect the comments

1 Draw lines to connect the marker's comments to the relevant parts of the student's answer. One has been done for you. Some comments may relate to more than one sentence in the student's answer.

3   (e)   Discuss the disadvantages to a business of being ethical.   (6)

Had a go

Ethics is doing what is thought to be morally correct.

This can mean paying a fair wage to employees.

It can also mean paying more for supplies that are

from sustainable sources. This will reduce the profits

of a business.

A correct disadvantage is given, but it is not clearly flagged up to the examiner as the main part of the argument.

The student shows knowledge.

The student jumps to the end of the argument without presenting a logical chain of reasoning.

Examples are used to show understanding.

When writing an extended answer, I try to remember to start with a relevant point and then fully develop this with a number of linked strands.

Hint
When a student makes a point that is relevant to the real world, rather than information taken from the extract, this is seen as showing their own knowledge of business.

Mark the answer

1 Use the mark scheme below to assign a mark to the student's answer on page 55.
Explain your decision.

Level	Mark	Descriptor
	0	No rewardable material.
Level 1	1–2	• Demonstrates elements of knowledge and understanding of business concepts and issues, with limited business terminology used (AO1b). • Attempts to deconstruct business information and/or issues, finding limited connections between points (AO3a).
Level 2	3–4	• Demonstrates more accurate knowledge and understanding of business concepts and issues, including appropriate use of business terminology in places (AO1b). • Attempts to deconstruct business information and/or issues, finding interconnected points with chain of reasoning, although there may be some logical inconsistencies (AO3a).
Level 3	5–6	• Demonstrates accurate knowledge and understanding of business concepts and issues, including appropriate use of business terminology (AO1b). • Deconstructs business information and/or issues, finding detailed interconnected points with logical chains of reasoning (AO3a).

I would award this student's answer .... out of 6 marks because ....

....

....

....

....

....

....

....

I always try to leave time at the end of an exam to go back and check what I have written. Sometimes I find a silly mistake or realise I need to add another sentence to develop my explanation.

Case study

The UK supermarket industry is very competitive. Some businesses, such as Marks & Spencer, compete by selling groceries that are seen to be of a superior quality. Others, such as Aldi and Lidl, compete by charging low prices.

In 2019, two of the largest supermarkets, Asda and Sainsbury's, discussed merging. Between them they own over 2000 shops. These include large out-of-town supermarkets plus smaller convenience stores owned by Sainsbury's, Sainsbury's Local. The supermarkets claim that the merger would allow them to reduce prices across all of their stores.

Aldi, a budget supermarket, has grown rapidly in the UK. In 2018 it opened eight new stores in one day. Aldi plans to have over 1000 stores in the UK by 2022, creating over 8000 new jobs. In 2019 Aldi opened its first convenience store to compete with Sainsbury's Local and Tesco Express. These are smaller stores located in, or close to, town and city centres.

In 2019, a chain of French budget supermarkets, Bonjour, moved into the UK market. They located themselves in out-of-town shopping areas, often close to Aldi or Lidl. Bonjour sells a range of fresh produce, such as breads and cakes cooked in store.

> **Hint**
> When reading the case study, underline or highlight information that you can use to answer the question. Where possible, building numbers into your answer is a good way to show context.

Improve the answer

1 Complete the student's answer so it would be awarded 2 marks.

---

4 (a) Outline **one** impact on Sainsbury's of an increase in competition. **(2)**

> **Hint**
> One impact has been identified. The question asks you to 'outline' one impact, so now you need to develop the answer to explain the stated impact. You only need one step in your development.

Nearly there

The customers will have more choice of where to shop.

....

....

....

....

....

---

2 Complete the student's answer so it would be awarded 2 marks.

---

4 (a) Outline **one** impact on Sainsbury's of an increase in competition. **(2)**

> **Hint**
> This time the supporting explanation has been identified, so you now need to identify the impact being explained.

Nearly there

The supermarket may be forced to ...., because shoppers will shop around

for the best deals. ....

....

Odd one out

1 Use the mark scheme below to decide which of these answers would **not** be awarded 2 marks. Explain your answer.

4 (a) Outline **one** benefit to Aldi of charging low prices. **(2)**

Question	Answer	Mark
4 (a)	Award up to 2 marks for linked points outlining a benefit to Aldi of charging low prices. Award a maximum of 1 mark if points are not linked.	2

A One benefit is Aldi will attract more customers. This will allow it to gain market share.

B Aldi will have a competitive advantage over larger supermarkets such as Sainsbury's. This will allow it to continue to grow.

C Aldi will benefit from positive word-of-mouth advertising. This is because customers will be satisfied with the low prices.

D Aldi will benefit from repeat customers. It will be able to offer a wide range of customer choice.

Student .... would not be awarded full marks because ....

....

....

....

....

....

Connect the comments

1 Draw lines to connect the marker's comments to the relevant parts of the student's answer. One has been done for you. Some comments may relate to more than one sentence in the student's answer.

---

4 (b) Analyse the benefit to Asda and Sainsbury's of a merger. **(6)**

Nearly there

The merger would allow the two supermarkets

to work together as one. This would give them

greater strength, with over 2000 stores

combined. This would allow them a lot of power

when negotiating prices with suppliers. They

could therefore gain stock at a lower cost.

This would allow them to charge lower prices

to their customers. This would mean they can

better compete with the increased number of

budget supermarkets, such as Aldi and Lidl.

A correct benefit has been identified, showing accurate knowledge. This clearly shows an understanding of one motive for a merger.

The student makes effective use of the context.

The student makes good use of the context to support their relevant point.

There are a number of developed points as to how Sainsbury's and Asda would benefit. The chain of reasoning is logical and methodically developed.

Hint
The more you get to know what examiners are looking for, the better your answers will become.

Mark the answer

1 Use the mark scheme below to assign a mark to the student's answer on page 60.
Explain your decision.

4   (b) Analyse the benefit to Asda and Sainsbury's of a merger.   **(6)**

Level	Mark	Descriptor
	0	No rewardable material.
Level 1	1–2	• Limited application of knowledge and understanding of business concepts and issues to the business context (AO2). • Attempts to deconstruct business information and/or issues, finding limited connections between points (AO3a).
Level 2	3–4	• Sound application of knowledge and understanding of business concepts and issues to the business context although there may be some inconsistencies (AO2). • Deconstructs business information and/or issues, finding interconnected points with chain of reasoning, although there may be some logical inconsistencies (AO3a).
Level 3	5–6	• Detailed application of knowledge and understanding of business concepts and issues to the business context throughout (AO2). • Deconstructs business information and/or issues, finding detailed interconnected points with logical chains of reasoning (AO3a).

I would award the student's answer .... out of 6 marks because ....

....

....

....

....

....

....

....

....

....

....

....

> **Hint**
> Always look at the number of marks available for a question. This gives a good indication of how much development is needed in the answer.

Complete the answer

1 Complete the student's answer so it would be awarded 2 marks.

Figure 1 shows the market research information taken from a budget supermarket in Corby.

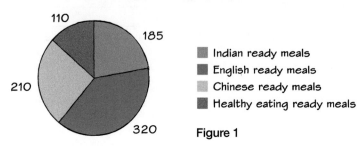

Average number of frozen ready meals sold in
a budget supermarket in Corby in one day

110
185
210
320

- Indian ready meals
- English ready meals
- Chinese ready meals
- Healthy eating ready meals

Figure 1

Hint
Pie charts represent portions
that add up to 100%. Read them
carefully and take note of labels
and/or keys.

5 (c) Using the information in **Figure 1**, calculate the number of Indian ready meals sold as a percentage of
all ready meals sold at the budget supermarket in Corby. You are advised to show your workings. **(2)**

Had a go

185 +

Hint
A percentage is one figure represented as a proportion of another. You must therefore
always identify two figures, divide one by the other and multiply by 100. It is important to
express your answer correctly by adding a % sign.

2 Complete the student's answer so it would be awarded 2 marks.

5 (c) Using the information in **Figure 1**, calculate the number of healthy ready meals sold as a percentage of
all ready meals sold at the budget supermarket in Corby. You are advised to show your workings. **(2)**

Nearly there

× 100 = 13%

Complete the answer

1 Complete the student's answer so it would be awarded 2 marks.

Figure 2 shows the market research information taken from a budget supermarket in Corby.

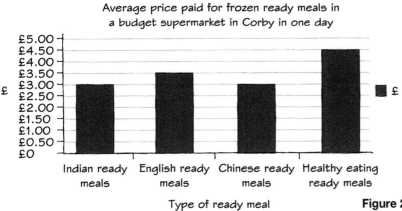

Average price paid for frozen ready meals in
a budget supermarket in Corby in one day

Hint
When reading information
from a bar chart, look
carefully at the chart
heading, axis labels and
key. It is important that you
read the information off the
chart accurately. You might
want to use a ruler to draw
a line from the top of the
bar to the axis, to ensure
you have read it properly.

Figure 2

5 (c) Using the information in **Figure 1** on page 62 and **Figure 2** above, calculate the average daily sales revenue
generated from Chinese ready meals at the budget supermarket in Corby. You are advised to show
your workings. **(2)**

Had a go

£3.00 ×..
....
....
....

2 Complete the student's answer so it would be awarded 2 marks.

5 (c) Using the information in **Figure 1** on page 62 and **Figure 2** above, calculate the average daily sales revenue
generated from English ready meals at the budget supermarket in Corby. You are advised to show
your workings. **(2)**

Nearly there

£3.50 ×..
....
....
....

Hint
Always show your workings. If you make a mistake but the examiner can see you were on the
right track, you may still be awarded a mark.

Improve the answer

1 Complete the student's answer so it would be awarded 6 marks.

Aldi offers 'Specialbuys' each week. These are a small number of goods, not normally stocked, offered at low prices.

5 (d) Analyse the advantage to Aldi of using special offers. **(6)**

> **Hint**
> One benefit has been identified. The question asks you to 'analyse' one impact, so now you need to develop the answer to analyse the stated benefit. You only need to develop a logical chain of reasoning in context.

Nearly there

One benefit is that this will attract customers on a weekly basis. This is because each week they will want to see what the new special offers are. This will encourage customers to visit the store more frequently.

I try to use a range of endings when developing my paragraphs. I do this by thinking in advance of the exam of a range of benefits that a business could enjoy. This way I avoid always saying 'leading to a rise in profit'. I think this makes my answers more in context, as I can think about what the specific business is trying to achieve.

Mark the answer

1 Find the correct answer. Choose **A**, **B** or **C**. Explain your choice.

6 (a) State **one** influence on the pricing strategy used by Aldi. **(1)**

Question	Answer	Mark
6 (a)	Award 1 mark for stating one influence on the pricing strategy used by Aldi. Do not accept strategies that do not apply to Aldi.	1

A   Low price

B   High price

C   Market segments

Answer .... would be awarded 1 mark because ....

....

....

2 Find the correct answer. Choose **A**, **B** or **C**. Explain your choice.

6 (a) State **one** way of working for sales assistants at Aldi. **(1)**

Question	Answer	Mark
6 (a)	Award 1 mark for stating one way of working for sales assistants at Aldi. Do not accept ways that are not suitable to Aldi.	1

A   Freelance contracts

B   Part-time

C   Remote working

Answer .... would be awarded 1 mark because ....

....

....

....

> When the command word is 'state', I try to answer the question using as few words as possible. There is no need to write in complete sentences. This saves me time so that I can make sure I do not run out of time on the higher mark questions.

Improve the answer

1 Complete the student's answer so it would be awarded 2 marks.

6 (b) Outline **one** advantage to Tesco of being a public limited company (PLC). **(2)**

> **Hint**
> One advantage has been identified. The question asks you to 'outline' one advantage, so now you need to develop the answer to explain the stated advantage. You only need one step in your development.

Nearly there

As a PLC, Tesco will be considered to be more prestigious and reliable.

....

....

....

....

....

2 Complete the student's answer so it would be awarded 2 marks.

6 (b) Outline **one** advantage to Tesco of being a public limited company (PLC). **(2)**

> **Hint**
> This time the supporting explanation has been identified, so you now need to identify the advantage being explained.

Nearly there

....

....

Therefore, it will have more power when negotiating with suppliers who want to be stocked

by the supermarket.

....

....

Build the answer

1 Look at the question and the list of ideas the student has extracted from the case study on page 57. The student has decided to choose option 1. Which ideas would you use in a plan to answer this question? Tick your top six pieces of information.

To achieve an objective of growth Bonjour is considering two options:

Option 1: Opening smaller stores in city centres

Option 2: Offering an e-commerce option allowing customers to have their shopping delivered

6 (c) Justify which **one** of these two options Bonjour should choose. **(9)**

> **Hint**
> Read through items A–I carefully before making your selection.

A	Tesco is a large competitor.	☐
B	This format has proved successful for larger supermarkets such as Tesco.	☐
C	Building an e-commerce site would be expensive.	☐
D	Consumers are increasingly looking for convenience.	☐
E	Aldi has just started doing this so Bonjour could follow the trend.	☐
F	Bonjour is new on the market but could use this to achieve growth.	☐
G	Bonjour is French.	☐
H	By locating in city centres, Bonjour could quickly become recognised even though it is new to the market.	☐
I	Bonjour sells a range of fresh produce such as breads and cakes cooked in store.	☐

2 Look at the items you have ticked. Choose **one** you would use in your argument **for** option 1. Justify your choice.

....

....

....

....

> **Hint**
> It is useful to note the number of marks a question is worth and break down your time accordingly.

Mark the answer

1 Use the mark scheme below to decide what mark you would give the student's answer to the question on page 67. Justify your decision.

Bonjour should open smaller stores in city centres. They are new to the UK market and this would allow them high visibility. This would mean that customers would try the new store when looking to buy food from a convenient location. Therefore, Bonjour would quickly gain a good reputation. This is because customers who try the freshly baked cakes are likely to go back, therefore allowing Bonjour to quickly gain a reputation. This could give them a competitive advantage over rivals Aldi.

Setting up a new e-commerce site is likely to be expensive. This is because Bonjour would have to build a website, buy delivery vans and employ drivers. It is unlikely that Bonjour would be able to compete against large competitors, such as Tesco, who already offer a delivery service. Therefore, this option would prove costly and is likely to fail.

Overall option 1 is the best, because it will allow Bonjour to achieve its objective of growth. The main reason for this is because customers who try the freshly baked goods are likely to become loyal to the brand.

Level	Mark	Descriptor
	0	No rewardable material.
Level 1	1–3	• Limited application of knowledge and understanding of business concepts and issues to the business context (AO2). • Attempts to deconstruct business information and/or issues, finding limited connections between points (AO3a). • Makes a judgement, providing a simple justification based on limited evaluation of business information and issues relevant to the choice made (AO3b).
Level 2	4–6	• Sound application of knowledge and understanding of business concepts and issues to the business context, although there may be some inconsistencies (AO2). • Deconstructs business information and/or issues, finding interconnected points with chain of reasoning, although there may be some logical inconsistencies (AO3a). • Makes a judgement, providing a justification based on sound evaluation of business information and issues relevant to the choice made (AO3b).
Level 3	7–9	• Detailed application of knowledge and understanding of business concepts and issues to the business context throughout (AO2). • Deconstructs business information and/or issues, finding detailed interconnected points with logical chains of reasoning (AO3a). • Makes a judgement, providing a clear justification based on a thorough evaluation of business information and issues relevant to the choice made (AO3b).

I would give this answer   out of 9 marks because

Case study

Heart Beat Ltd is a UK-based private limited company (Ltd). It was founded by father and son Robert and Mark. The business was first established using Robert's redundancy money from an engineering company he had worked at for 25 years. In 2016, Heart Beat Ltd grew rapidly, winning prestigious awards for product innovation at the 2018 Lifestyle Awards. A Heart Beat is a fitness band worn on your wrist, like a watch. It monitors physical activity and key data such as pulse, heart rate and calories burnt. In 2019, a Heart Beat was seen on the wrist of a top athlete at the World Athletics Championships.

In just three years, Heart Beat Ltd saw annual profits rise from £350 000 to £5 million.

The Heart Beat device currently sells for £99. In 2020, Heart Beat Ltd will launch a deluxe model – the Heart Beat Olympic tracker. As part of its promotion, the company has signed a sponsorship deal with the UK women's hockey team. The new device will have additional features, including GPS tracking, access to emails and personalised goal setting. It will sell for £249. A competitor sells a similar model for £350. A leading provider of life insurance has agreed a deal with Heart Beat Ltd that customers wearing the deluxe model can sync their data with the insurance company, earning up to 20% discount on life insurance.

> **Hint**
> As you revise key terms, it is helpful to think of a real-life example. Here, an example of a private limited company would be Virgin Atlantic.

Remember – you can annotate the case study texts as much as you want. I find it really helpful to underline key words and phrases.

Find the answer

1 Find the student's answer that would be awarded 1 mark. Choose **A, B, C** or **D**.
Explain your choice.

---

7 (a) Define the term private limited company. **(1)**

A A company that can sell shares on a stock exchange

B A company that sells a range of goods to members of the public

C A company that can sell shares to family and friends

D A company that is owned by just one person

Answer .... would be awarded 1 mark because ....

....

....

....

---

2 Find the student's answer that would be awarded 1 mark. Choose **A, B, C** or **D**.
Explain your choice.

---

7 (a) Define the term sponsorship. **(1)**

A Providing financial support for an event in return for brand exposure

B Paying a sports person to compete in a high profile event

C Advertising a brand in the media

D A promotional method used to raise awareness of a brand

Answer .... would be awarded one mark because ....

....

....

....

Find the answer

1 Find the student's answer that would be awarded 1 mark. Choose **A**, **B** or **C**. Explain your choice.

Figure 3 is a bar gate stock graph for Heart Beat Ltd.

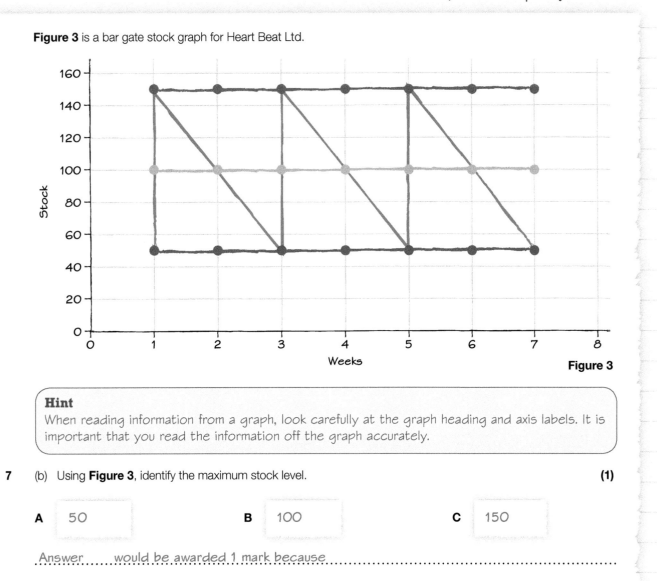

Figure 3

> **Hint**
> When reading information from a graph, look carefully at the graph heading and axis labels. It is important that you read the information off the graph accurately.

7 (b) Using **Figure 3**, identify the maximum stock level. **(1)**

| **A** | 50 | **B** | 100 | **C** | 150 |

Answer .... would be awarded 1 mark because ....

....

2 Find the student's answer that would be awarded 1 mark. Choose **A**, **B**, **C** or **D**. Explain your choice.

7 (b) When the stock level reaches 100, stock is automatically reordered. Using **Figure 3**, identify how long it takes for stock to be delivered. **(1)**

| **A** | 50 units | **B** | 100 units | **C** | 1 week | **D** | 2 weeks |

Answer .... would be awarded 1 mark because ....

....

....

Connect the comments

1 Draw lines to connect the marker's comments to the relevant parts of the student's answer. One has been done for you. Some comments may relate to more than one sentence in the student's answer.

> **Hint**
> This is just the first paragraph of the student's answer – it is not the whole answer.

Heart Beat Ltd needs to raise finance to develop the Heart Beat Olympic tracker. It is considering the following two options:

Option 1: Becoming a public limited company

Option 2: Using retained profit

7 (d) Justify which **one** of these two options Heart Beat Ltd should choose. **(9)**

Nailed it!

Robert and Mark should choose option 2.
This is because they are a father-and-son
team, so would not want to lose control of the
business. In just three years there was a rapid
increase in profits to £5 million. This implies
that they could afford to fund the research and
development of the new tracker from existing
profit levels. This will allow Robert and Mark to
maintain 100% control of the business – which is
what they want to do as it is a family business.

The student starts with a clear statement telling the examiner that this paragraph is going to look at why using retained profit is the best option.

The student shows good use of business terminology to explain how the retained profit could be used.

The paragraph is then developed with a number of interconnected points showing a logical chain of reasoning.

The student makes good use of the data in the extract to argue why Robert and Mark can afford to fund the new product development through retained profit.

The student supports their decision by considering the negative of the alternative option.

Re-order the answer

1 The sentences below are taken from a paragraph written by a student in response to the following question. Rearrange the sentences into the most logical order by numbering them 1 to 8.

7 (e) Evaluate the importance of quality to Heart Beat Ltd. You should use the information provided as well as your knowledge of business. **(12)**

> **Hint**
> It's important that answers to this type of question are in a logical order. Make sure you read your answer through from the start to check it makes sense.

.... Otherwise, there will be complaints. ....

....

.... Quality is important to Heart Beat because a poor-quality product could damage ....

.... its reputation. ....

....

.... This would be very dangerous, as this is a competitive market with big businesses, ...

.... such as Apple and Fitbit, that have a large share of the market. ....

....

.... This is especially true as Heart Beat is bringing out a luxury version of its fitness ....

.... tracker. ....

....

.... Leading to a loss of their competitive advantage. ....

....

.... Therefore, to warrant a high price of £249 it will have to be of good quality. ....

....

.... This means that it must fulfil all of the functions such as allowing emails effectively. ....

....

.... This would mean that other businesses such as the insurance company, would not ....

.... want to work with them. ....

....

When I read the extract, I try to identify other businesses that I know operate in the same market. This helps me bring my own knowledge of business into my answers.

Mark the answer

1 Use the mark scheme below to decide what mark you would give the student's answer. Justify your decision. The whole answer is the rearranged answer on page 73 plus the following two paragraphs. Look back at page 73 to remind yourself of the main points.

7 (e) Evaluate the importance of quality to Heart Beat Ltd. You should use the information provided as well as your knowledge of business. **(12)**

> **Hint**
> 12-mark 'Evaluate' questions require an extended response with a number of steps in a line of reasoning on context. It is important to try to use business terminology within your line of reasoning as well as specific information from the extract provided. The analytical paragraphs should lead to a fully supported conclusion based on the context provided.

Quality is also important, as this will allow Heart Beat to control costs. This is an important part of the design mix alongside function and aesthetics. If there are quality issues then goods will be faulty, leading to high wastage costs to either scrap or make the trackers. This would push costs up, meaning that Heart Beat would see a fall in profit margins. Their Heart Beat Olympic tracker is competitively priced at £249, which is cheaper than rivals who charge £350. This is an important competitive advantage to Heart Beat, who may not have the brand loyalty of other businesses in the market. This is important, as Heart Beat may be targeting customers who cannot afford the alternatives. These customers are more aware of prices and would also be attracted by the discount on the life insurance. This could be especially true in the UK at the moment, where there are high levels of uncertainty about the economy.

Overall, I think quality is very important to Heart Beat. The main reason for this is that customers will want a product that lasts and can be trusted to carry out all of the functions that Heart Beat says it does.

Level	Mark	Descriptor
	0	No rewardable material.
Level 1	1–4	• Demonstrates elements of knowledge and understanding of business concepts and issues, with limited business terminology used (AO1b). • Limited application of knowledge and understanding of business concepts and issues to the business context (AO2). • Attempts to deconstruct business information and/or issues, finding limited connections between points (AO3a). • Draws a conclusion, supported by generic assertions from limited evaluation of business information and issues (AO3b).
Level 2	5–8	• Demonstrates mostly accurate knowledge and understanding of business concepts and issues, including appropriate use of business terminology in places (AO1b). • Sound application of knowledge and understanding of business concepts and issues to the business context, although there may be some inconsistencies (AO2). • Deconstructs business information and/or issues, finding interconnected points with chains of reasoning, although there may be some logical inconsistencies (AO3a). • Draws a conclusion based on sound evaluation of business information and issues (AO3b).
Level 3	9–12	• Demonstrates accurate knowledge and understanding of business concepts and issues throughout, including appropriate use of business terminology (AO1b). • Detailed application of knowledge and understanding of business concepts and issues to the business context throughout (AO2). • Deconstructs business information and/or issues, finding detailed interconnected points with logical chains of reasoning (AO3a). • Draws a valid and well-reasoned conclusion based on a thorough evaluation of business information and issues (AO3b).

I would give the student's answer ...... out of 12 marks because ....

....

....

....

....

....

....

....

....

....

Where an example answer is given, this is not necessarily the only correct response. In most cases, there is a range of responses that can gain full marks.

In questions that have more than one correct answer, you will see the (Suggested answer) stamp.

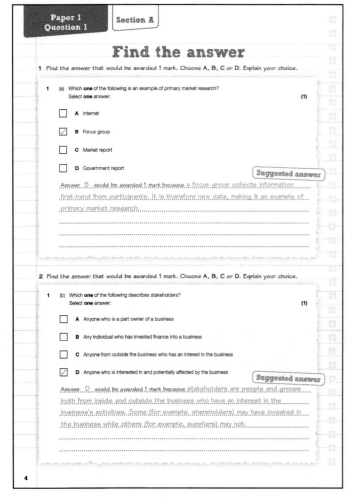

Paper 1 Question 1 | **Section A**

Find the answer

1 Find the answer that would be awarded 1 mark. Choose A, B, C or D. Explain your choice.

1 (a) Which **one** of the following is an example of primary market research?
Select **one** answer: (1)

☐ A Internet

☑ B Focus group

☐ C Market report

☐ D Government report

(Suggested answer)

Answer B would be awarded 1 mark because a focus group collects information first-hand from participants. It is therefore new data, making it an example of primary market research.

2 Find the answer that would be awarded 1 mark. Choose A, B, C or D. Explain your choice.

1 (b) Which **one** of the following describes stakeholders?
Select **one** answer: (1)

☐ A Anyone who is a part owner of a business

☐ B Any individual who has invested finance into a business

☐ C Anyone from outside the business who has an interest in the business

☑ D Anyone who is interested in and potentially affected by the business

(Suggested answer)

Answer D would be awarded 1 mark because stakeholders are people and groups both from inside and outside the business who have an interest in the business's activities. Some (for example, shareholders) may have invested in the business while others (for example, suppliers) may not.

4

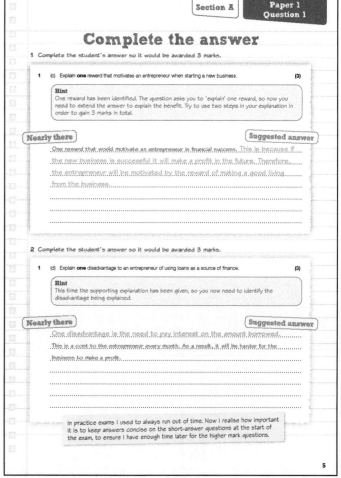

Section A | **Paper 1 Question 1**

Complete the answer

1 Complete the student's answer so it would be awarded 3 marks.

1 (c) Explain **one** reward that motivates an entrepreneur when starting a new business. (3)

Hint
One reward has been identified. The question asks you to 'explain' one reward, so now you need to extend the answer to explain the benefit. Try to use two steps in your explanation in order to gain 3 marks in total.

(Nearly there) (Suggested answer)

One reward that would motivate an entrepreneur is financial success. This is because if the new business is successful it will make a profit in the future. Therefore, the entrepreneur will be motivated by the reward of making a good living from the business.

2 Complete the student's answer so it would be awarded 3 marks.

1 (d) Explain **one** disadvantage to an entrepreneur of using loans as a source of finance. (3)

Hint
This time the supporting explanation has been given, so you now need to identify the disadvantage being explained.

(Nearly there) (Suggested answer)

One disadvantage is the need to pay interest on the amount borrowed. This is a cost to the entrepreneur every month. As a result, it will be harder for the business to make a profit.

In practice exams I used to always run out of time. Now I realise how important it is to keep answers concise on the short-answer questions at the start of the exam, to ensure I have enough time later for the higher mark questions.

5

Panel 1 (page 6)

Improve the answer

1 Use the hints below to write an improved answer to this question.

> 1 (c) Explain **one** role of an entrepreneur when setting up a business. (3)
>
> **Hint**
> Remember, for 3-mark 'Explain' questions there is 1 mark for stating a correct point, in this case a role. The further 2 marks are awarded for explaining that point.
>
> **Hint**
> Use connectives such as 'this means that', 'which will lead to' and 'therefore', etc, to help you develop your explanations.

Had a go / **Suggested answer**

Making business decisions. This means the entrepreneur decides what products or services to sell and at what price. In this way, the entrepreneur helps the business meet the needs of its customers.

> I always start my answers with a relevant point or piece of theory from the specification. To help me do this I use the specification when revising.

2 Use the hints above to write an improved answer to this question.

> 1 (d) Explain the importance of cash to a business. (3)

Nearly there

One reason why cash is important is because it will allow the business to meet day-to-day expenses. This will allow it to buy new supplies, pay wages and utility bills. As a result, the business will be able to continue to trade, as it has the necessary resources. **Suggested answer**

Panel 2 (page 7)

Complete the question

1 Complete the question by adding three multiple choice options. Make sure two are correct.

> **Hint**
> Multiple choice questions often have answers that are believable but incorrect. These are called distractors. Try to make it relatively difficult to spot the incorrect answer.

> 2 (a) Which **two** of the following are examples of non-financial business objectives?
> Select **two** answers. (2)
>
> ☐ A Market share
> ☑ B Social objectives
> ☑ C Personal satisfaction
> ☐ D Sales   **Suggested answer**
> ☐ E Profit

2 Complete the question by adding three multiple choice options. Make sure two are correct.

> 2 (b) Which **two** of the following are examples of short-term sources of finance?
> Select **two** answers. (2)
>
> ☐ A Share capital
> ☑ B Overdraft
> ☐ C Crowdfunding   **Suggested answer**
> ☐ D Retained profit
> ☑ E Trade credit

Panel 3 (page 8)

Find the answer

1 Find the answer that would be awarded 2 marks. Choose A, B or C. Explain your choice.

Table 1 contains information about a small business for its first year. The business sold 10 000 units in this year.

Fixed costs	£20000
Variable costs (per unit)	£6.50
Selling price (per unit)	£9.00

Table 1

2 (c) Using the information in **Table 1**, calculate the break-even output for this business. You are advised to show your workings. (2)

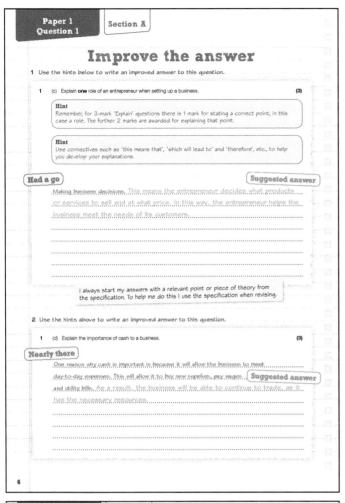

A $\frac{10\,000\text{ units}}{(£9.00 - £6.50)} = \frac{10\,000\text{ units}}{(£2.50)} = 4000$ units

> I always show my workings, because even if the answer is wrong, I might get some marks.

B $\frac{£20\,000}{(£9.00 - £6.50)} = \frac{£20\,000}{(£2.50)} = 8000$ units

> **Hint**
> Always check your answer. It is very easy in exam conditions to press a wrong number on your calculator.

C $\frac{£9.00 \times 10\,000}{£20\,000} = \frac{£90\,000}{£20\,000} = 4500$ units

Suggested answer

Answer B would be awarded 2 marks because break-even is calculated using the formula fixed costs divided by (selling price per unit — variable costs per unit).

2 Find the answer that would be awarded 2 marks. Choose A, B or C. Explain your choice.

Table 2 shows the cash flow forecast for a small business.

2 (c) Complete **Table 2** with the two missing figures. (2)

	Month 1 (£)	Month 2 (£)
Cash inflows	28500	30800
Cash outflows	31000	(ii) ....
Net cash flow	(i)	3000
Opening balance	5000	2500
Closing balance	2500	5500

Table 2

A i = (2500), ii = 33800   B i = (2500), ii = 27800

C i = 2500, ii = 27800

Suggested answer

Answer A would be awarded 2 marks because (i) Net cash flow = cash inflows — cash outflows, and (ii) Cash outflows = cash inflows + net cash flow

---

Panel 4 (page 9)

Improve the answer

1 Use the hints below to write an improved answer to this question.

> 2 (d) Explain **one** benefit to a new business of starting as a franchise. (3)
>
> **Hint**
> Remember, for 3-mark 'Explain' questions there is 1 mark for stating a correct point, in this case a benefit. The further 2 marks are for explaining this benefit.

Had a go / **Suggested answer**

Support from the franchisor. This means that the entrepreneur will be given advice on issues such as cash flow management, therefore reducing the risk to an inexperienced entrepreneur of failure.

> I used to just focus on learning advantages and disadvantages. Now I practise developing why each point is an advantage or a disadvantage. This has really helped me gain confidence.

2 Use the hints below to write an improved answer to this question.

> 2 (e) Explain **one** purpose of producing a business plan. (3)

Nearly there

One purpose is it will make it easier for an entrepreneur to obtain finance. This is because it can show a bank manager the forecast cash flow. As a result, they will be more confident of the entrepreneur's ability to repay a loan. **Suggested answer**

Complete the question

1 Complete the question by adding three multiple choice options. Make sure only one is correct.

3 (a) Which **one** of the following is an advantage of being a private limited company?
Select **one** answer. (1)

- [ ] A Retained profit
- [x] B Limited liability
- [ ] C Limited sources of finance
- [ ] D Established brand name

Suggested answer

2 Complete the question by adding four multiple choice options. Make sure only one is correct.

3 (a) Which **one** of the following is an example of the impact of technology on the marketing mix?
Select **one** answer. (1)

- [ ] A Price
- [ ] B Payment methods
- [x] C e-commerce
- [ ] D Place

Suggested answer

Hint
When answering a multiple choice question, is important to read all of the options carefully. The examiner will often include an answer that is quite close to the correct one. If you cross through the answers you know are wrong first, this will help you to narrow down the correct answer.

3 Complete the question by adding four multiple choice options. Make sure only one is correct.

3 (a) Which one of the following is a type of organisational structure?
Select **one** answer. (1)

- [ ] A Supervisor
- [x] B Hierarchical
- [ ] C Communication
- [ ] D Remote working

Suggested answer

Improve the answer

1 Write an improved answer that would be awarded full marks.

Figure 1 shows the change in the profit of a business over three months.

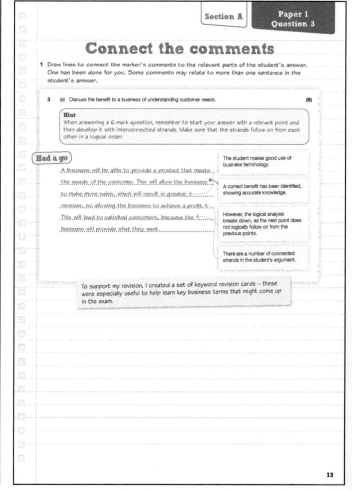

Profit

January 1500 — February 2200 — March 2800

£ (axis 0 to 3000)

Month

☐ Profit (£)

Figure 1

Hint
Remember that the information presented in graphs will be stated on each axis. It is important to read the axis carefully.

3 (b) Using the information in **Figure 1**, calculate the percentage increase in profit between January and March.
You are advised to show your workings. (2)

Hint
When calculating the percentage difference between two numbers, use the percentage change calculation. Remember the formula is: $\frac{change}{original} \times 100$. Don't forget the × 100 to express your answer as a percentage.

£2800
− £1500
= £1300

$\frac{£1300}{£1500} \times 100 = 87\%$

Suggested answer

When I was revising for my exams, I tried all of the 'Calculate' questions over and over again. I would sometimes change the numbers in the question, just so I had new numbers to practise with. I would then ask someone to check my answers for me.

Mark the answer

1 Use the marking instructions below to decide how many marks you would award this student's answer.

3 (c) Explain **one** benefit to consumers of consumer law. (3)

Had a go

One benefit of consumer law in that the customer has the right to return goods that are faulty. This means that the customer will not have wasted money. This also means that the business must disclose all information about a product to the customer.

Question	Answer	Mark
3 (c)	Award 1 mark for identification of a benefit, plus 2 further marks for explaining this benefit up to a total of 3 marks. Answers that list more than one benefit with no explanation will be awarded a maximum of 1 mark.	3

I would award this student's answer 2 out of 3 marks because the student has identified a relevant benefit (that the consumer has the right to return faulty goods), which is then developed with one further step (the benefit of this is that the customer has not wasted their money). However, the student then goes on to give a second benefit, rather than fully developing the explanation of their first point.

Suggested answer

When I first started practising exam-style questions, I would try and write down everything I knew about a topic. For example, if I had learned four benefits to the consumer of consumer law, I wrote about all of them. Now I have learned to be strict with myself on the lower mark questions and state just one benefit, which I then develop. This approach has saved me a lot of time and improved my marks.

Connect the comments

1 Draw lines to connect the marker's comments to the relevant parts of the student's answer. One has been done for you. Some comments may relate to more than one sentence in the student's answer.

3 (e) Discuss the benefit to a business of understanding customer needs. (6)

Hint
When answering a 6-mark question, remember to start your answer with a relevant point and then develop it with interconnected strands. Make sure that the strands follow on from each other in a logical order.

Had a go

A business will be able to provide a product that meets the needs of the customer. This will allow the business to make more sales, which will result in greater revenue, so allowing the business to achieve a profit. This will lead to satisfied customers, because the business will provide what they want.

The student makes good use of business terminology.

A correct benefit has been identified, showing accurate knowledge.

However, the logical analysis breaks down, as the next point does not logically follow on from the previous points.

There are a number of connected strands in the student's argument.

To support my revision, I created a set of keyword revision cards – these were especially useful to help learn key business terms that might come up in the exam.

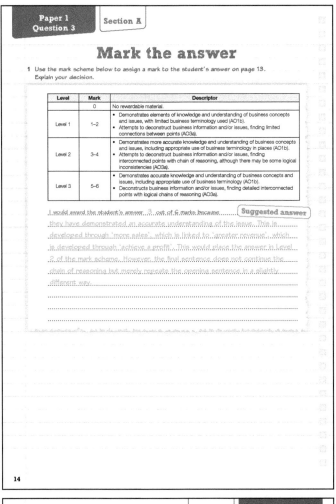

Mark the answer

1 Use the mark scheme below to assign a mark to the student's answer on page 13. Explain your decision.

Level	Mark	Descriptor
	0	No rewardable material.
Level 1	1–2	• Demonstrates elements of knowledge and understanding of business concepts and issues, with limited business terminology used (AO1b). • Attempts to deconstruct business information and/or issues, finding limited connections between points (AO3a).
Level 2	3–4	• Demonstrates more accurate knowledge and understanding of business concepts and issues, including appropriate use of business terminology in places (AO1b). • Attempts to deconstruct business information and/or issues, finding interconnected points with chain of reasoning, although there may be some logical inconsistencies (AO3a).
Level 3	5–6	• Demonstrates accurate knowledge and understanding of business concepts and issues, including appropriate use of business terminology (AO1b). • Deconstructs business information and/or issues, finding detailed interconnected points with logical chains of reasoning (AO3a).

Suggested answer

I would award the student's answer 3 out of 6 marks because they have demonstrated an accurate understanding of the issue. This is developed through 'more sales', which is linked to 'greater revenue', which is developed through 'achieve a profit'. This would place the answer in Level 2 of the mark scheme. However, the final sentence does not continue the chain of reasoning but merely repeats the opening sentence in a slightly different way.

14

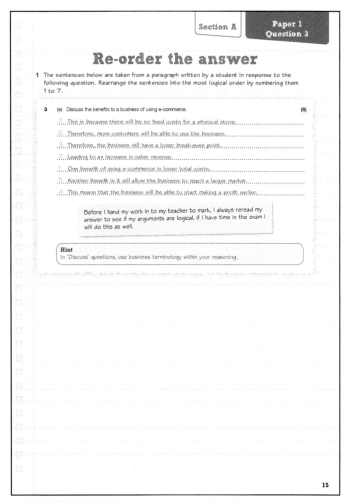

Re-order the answer

1 The sentences below are taken from a paragraph written by a student in response to the following question. Rearrange the sentences into the most logical order by numbering them 1 to 7.

3 (e) Discuss the benefits to a business of using e-commerce. (6)

2 This is because there will be no fixed costs for a physical store.

6 Therefore, more customers will be able to use the business.

3 Therefore, the business will have a lower break-even point.

7 Leading to an increase in sales revenue.

1 One benefit of using e-commerce is lower total costs.

5 Another benefit is it will allow the business to reach a larger market.

4 This means that the business will be able to start making a profit earlier.

Before I hand my work in to my teacher to mark, I always reread my answer to see if my arguments are logical. If I have time in the exam I will do this as well.

Hint

In 'Discuss' questions, use business terminology within your reasoning.

15

Odd one out

1 Use the mark scheme below to decide which of these answers would **not** be awarded 2 marks. Explain your answer.

4 (a) Outline **one** market segment that Brad could target with his brand of cycle wear, Moser. (2)

Question	Answer	Mark
4 (a)	Award up to 2 marks for linked points outlining a suitable market segment for Moser. Award a maximum of 1 mark if points are not linked.	2

A People with a healthy lifestyle are a suitable market segment because the cycle wear is designed to be functional when cycling as a sporting activity.

B Teenagers are a market segment because they will want cycle wear that is also fashionable.

C One suitable market segment is parents of students who are studying at university, because they will want their child to have good-quality lights when cycling.

D One suitable market segment is young professionals, because they will want a good-quality range of cycle wear that is also fashionable.

Suggested answer

Student C would not be awarded full marks because the answer links to the accessories sold by Brad Bikes and not the brand of cycle wear, Moser, as specified in the question.

I use a highlighter when reading the question, to underline the business term and also the reference to the extract. For example, in the question above I would highlight 'market segment' as the business term and 'brand of cycle wear' as the reference to the extract. This helps me to make sure I am answering the precise question.

Hint

Always look at the number of marks available for a question. This gives a good indication of how much development is needed in the answer.

17

Complete the answer

1 Complete the student's answer so it would be awarded 6 marks.

4 (b) Brad is keen to build his brand Moser using digital communication. Analyse the benefit to Brad of using digital communication. (6)

Hint

One benefit has been identified. The question asks you to 'analyse' the benefit, so now you need to develop the answer. The command word analyse requires detailed interconnected points.

Nearly there

One benefit of using digital communication is that social media is popular with young people. This will allow Brad to promote his brand with images of cyclists wearing his goods. This will be shared by followers, allowing it to reach a wider target market.

Suggested answer

This will make more customers aware of the new brand, therefore growing the reputation of the business. This will mean an increase in sales revenue, which will allow Brad to invest further in developing his brand.

When given additional information at the start of a question, I always try to include this in my answer. It helps me to plan where my answer is going to end.

18

Answers

Connect the comments

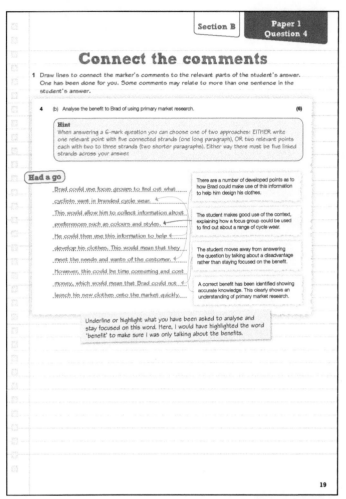

1 Draw lines to connect the marker's comments to the relevant parts of the student's answer. One has been done for you. Some comments may relate to more than one sentence in the student's answer.

4 (b) Analyse the benefit to Brad of using primary market research. **(6)**

Hint
When answering a 6-mark question you can choose one of two approaches: EITHER write one relevant point with five connected strands (one long paragraph), OR two relevant points each with two to three strands (two shorter paragraphs). Either way there must be five linked strands across your answer.

Had a go

Brad could use focus groups to find out what cyclists want in branded cycle wear. This would allow him to collect information about preferences such as colours and style. He could then use this information to help develop his clothes. This would mean that they meet the needs and wants of the customer. However, this could be time consuming and cost money, which would mean that Brad could not launch his new clothes onto the market quickly.

There are a number of developed points as to how Brad could make use of this information to help him design his clothes.

The student makes good use of the context, explaining how a focus group could be used to find out about a range of cycle wear.

The student moves away from answering the question by talking about a disadvantage rather than staying focused on the benefit.

A correct benefit has been identified showing accurate knowledge. This clearly shows an understanding of primary market research.

Underline or highlight what you have been asked to analyse and stay focused on this word. Here, I would have highlighted the word 'benefit' to make sure I was only talking about the benefits.

19

Mark the answer

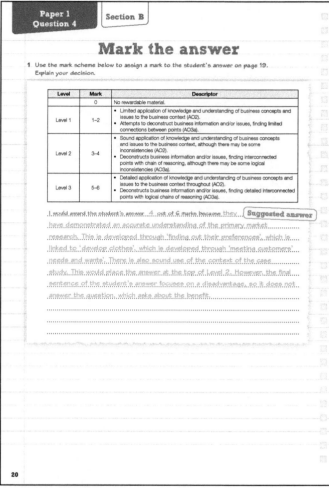

1 Use the mark scheme below to assign a mark to the student's answer on page 19. Explain your decision.

Level	Mark	Descriptor
	0	No rewardable material.
Level 1	1–2	• Limited application of knowledge and understanding of business concepts and issues to the business context (AO2). • Attempts to deconstruct business information and/or issues, finding limited connections between points (AO3a).
Level 2	3–4	• Sound application of knowledge and understanding of business concepts and issues to the business context, although there may be some inconsistencies (AO2). • Deconstructs business information and/or issues, finding interconnected points with chain of reasoning, although there may be some logical inconsistencies (AO3a).
Level 3	5–6	• Detailed application of knowledge and understanding of business concepts and issues to the business context throughout (AO2). • Deconstructs business information and/or issues, finding detailed interconnected points with logical chains of reasoning (AO3a).

Suggested answer

I would award the student's answer 4 out of 6 marks because they have demonstrated an accurate understanding of the primary market research. This is developed through 'finding out their preferences', which is linked to 'develop clothes', which is developed through 'meeting customers' needs and wants'. There is also sound use of the context of the case study. This would place the answer at the top of Level 2. However, the final sentence of the student's answer focuses on a disadvantage, so it does not answer the question, which asks about the benefit.

20

Find the answer

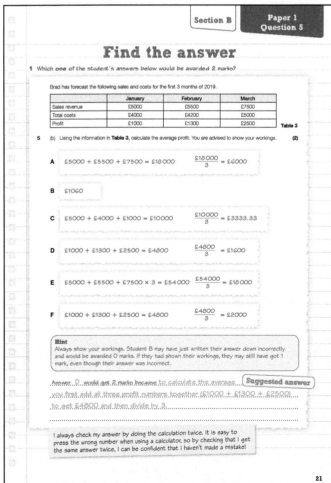

1 Which **one** of the student's answers below would be awarded 2 marks?

Brad has forecast the following sales and costs for the first 3 months of 2019.

	January	February	March
Sales revenue	£5000	£5500	£7500
Total costs	£4000	£4200	£5000
Profit	£1000	£1300	£2500

Table 3

5 (b) Using the information in **Table 3**, calculate the average profit. You are advised to show your workings. **(2)**

A £5000 + £5500 + £7500 = £18 000 $\frac{£18\,000}{3}$ = £6000

B £1060

C £5000 + £4000 + £1000 = £10 000 $\frac{£10\,000}{3}$ = £3333.33

D £1000 + £1300 + £2500 = £4800 $\frac{£4800}{3}$ = £1600

E £5000 + £5500 + £7500 × 3 = £54 000 $\frac{£54\,000}{3}$ = £18 000

F £1000 + £1300 + £2500 = £4800 $\frac{£4800}{3}$ = £2000

Hint
Always show your workings. Student B may have just written their answer down incorrectly and would be awarded 0 marks. If they had shown their workings, they may still have got 1 mark, even though their answer was incorrect.

Suggested answer
Answer D would get 2 marks because to calculate the average you first add all three profit numbers together (£1000 + £1300 + £2500) to get £4800 and then divide by 3.

I always check my answer by doing the calculation twice. It is easy to press the wrong number when using a calculator, so by checking that I get the same answer twice, I can be confident that I haven't made a mistake!

21

Complete the question

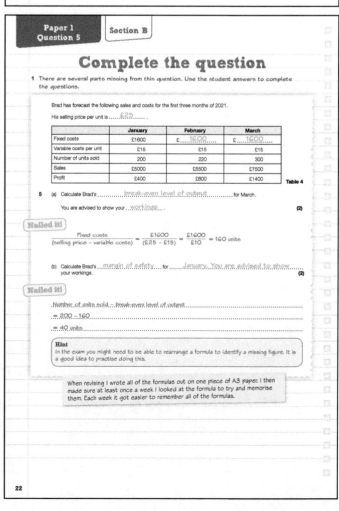

1 There are several parts missing from this question. Use the student answers to complete the questions.

Brad has forecast the following sales and costs for the first three months of 2021.

His selling price per unit is ...... £25 ......

	January	February	March
Fixed costs	£1600	£ 1600	£ 1600
Variable costs per unit	£15	£15	£15
Number of units sold	200	220	300
Sales	£5000	£5500	£7500
Profit	£400	£800	£1400

Table 4

5 (a) Calculate Brad's ...... break-even level of output ...... for March.

You are advised to show your ...... workings ...... **(2)**

Nailed it!

$\frac{\text{Fixed costs}}{(\text{selling price} - \text{variable costs})} = \frac{£1600}{(£25 - £15)} = \frac{£1600}{£10} = 160$ units

(b) Calculate Brad's ...... margin of safety ...... for ...... January. You are advised to show your workings. **(2)**

Nailed it!

Number of units sold − break-even level of output

= 200 − 160

= 40 units

Hint
In the exam you might need to be able to rearrange a formula to identify a missing figure. It is a good idea to practise doing this.

When revising I wrote all of the formulas out on one piece of A3 paper. I then made sure at least once a week I looked at the formula to try and memorise them. Each week it got easier to remember all of the formulas.

22

80

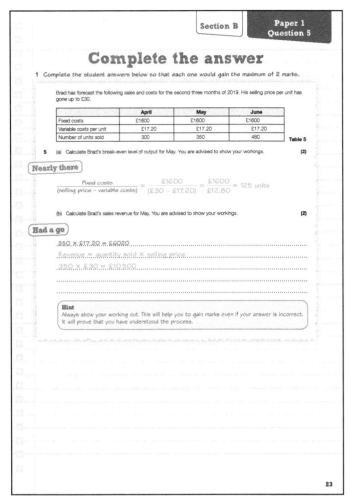

Complete the answer

1 Complete the student answers below so that each one would gain the maximum of 2 marks.

Brad has forecast the following sales and costs for the second three months of 2019. His selling price per unit has gone up to £30.

	April	May	June
Fixed costs	£1600	£1600	£1600
Variable costs per unit	£17.20	£17.20	£17.20
Number of units sold	300	350	480

Table 5

5 (a) Calculate Brad's break-even level of output for May. You are advised to show your workings. (2)

Nearly there

$$\frac{Fixed\ costs}{(selling\ price - variable\ costs)} = \frac{£1600}{(£30 - £17.20)} = \frac{£1600}{£12.80} = 125\ units$$

(b) Calculate Brad's sales revenue for May. You are advised to show your workings. (2)

Had a go

350 × £17.20 = £6020

Revenue = quantity sold × selling price

350 × £30 = £10,500

Hint
Always show your working out. This will help you to gain marks even if your answer is incorrect. It will prove that you have understood the process.

23

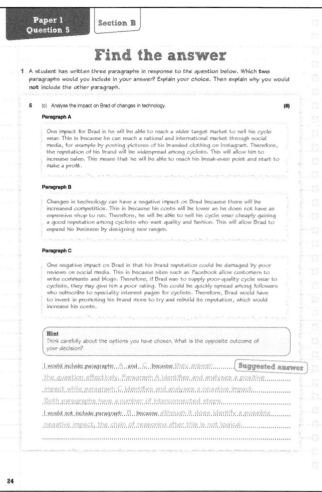

Find the answer

1 A student has written three paragraphs in response to the question below. Which **two** paragraphs would you include in your answer? Explain your choice. Then explain why you would **not** include the other paragraph.

5 (c) Analyse the impact on Brad of changes in technology. (6)

Paragraph A

One impact for Brad is he will be able to reach a wider target market to sell his cycle wear. This is because he can reach a national and international market through social media, for example by posting pictures of his branded clothing on Instagram. Therefore, the reputation of his brand will be widespread among cyclists. This will allow him to increase sales. This means that he will be able to reach his break-even point and start to make a profit.

Paragraph B

Changes in technology can have a negative impact on Brad because there will be increased competition. This is because his costs will be lower as he does not have an expensive shop to run. Therefore, he will be able to sell his cycle wear cheaply gaining a good reputation among cyclists who want quality and fashion. This will allow Brad to expand his business by designing new ranges.

Paragraph C

One negative impact on Brad is that his brand reputation could be damaged by poor reviews on social media. This is because sites such as Facebook allow customers to write comments and blogs. Therefore, if Brad was to supply poor-quality cycle wear to cyclists, they may give him a poor rating. This could be quickly spread among followers who subscribe to speciality interest pages for cyclists. Therefore, Brad would have to invest in promoting his brand more to try and rebuild its reputation, which would increase his costs.

Hint
Think carefully about the options you have chosen. What is the opposite outcome of your decision?

I would include paragraphs A and C because they answer **Suggested answer** the question effectively. Paragraph A identifies and analyses a positive impact while paragraph C identifies and analyses a negative impact. Both paragraphs have a number of interconnected steps. I would not include paragraph B because, although it does identify a possible negative impact, the chain of reasoning after this is not logical.

24

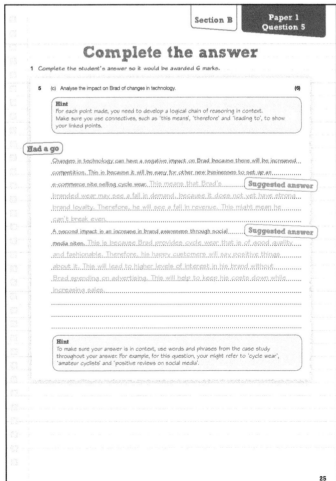

Complete the answer

1 Complete the student's answer so it would be awarded 6 marks.

5 (c) Analyse the impact on Brad of changes in technology. (6)

Hint
For each point made, you need to develop a logical chain of reasoning in context. Make sure you use connectives, such as 'this means', 'therefore' and 'leading to', to show your linked points.

Had a go

Changes in technology can have a negative impact on Brad because there will be increased competition. This is because it will be easy for other new businesses to set up an e-commerce site selling cycle wear. This means that Brad's **Suggested answer** branded wear may see a fall in demand, because it does not yet have strong brand loyalty. Therefore, he will see a fall in revenue. This might mean he can't break even.

A second impact is an increase in brand awareness through social **Suggested answer** media sites. This is because Brad provides cycle wear that is of good quality and fashionable. Therefore, his happy customers will say positive things about it. This will lead to higher levels of interest in his brand without Brad spending on advertising. This will help to keep his costs down while increasing sales.

Hint
To make sure your answer is in context, use words and phrases from the case study throughout your answer. For example, for this question, your might refer to 'cycle wear', 'amateur cyclists' and 'positive reviews on social media'.

25

Mark the answer

1 Read the six student answers shown below.
(a) Which three would you award 1 mark to? Explain your answer.
(b) Which three would you not award a mark to? Explain your answer.

6 (a) State **one** impact on Brad of increased competition. (1)

Question	Answer	Mark
6 (a)	Award 1 mark for stating one impact on Brad of increased competition. Do not award marks for impacts that would not be appropriate for Brad.	1

A | Brad would see a fall in sales.

B | Lower revenue from selling branded cycle wear.

C | Lower profits, as customers will go elsewhere.

D | Brad would need to keep his shop open for longer to attract customers.

E | Brad would need to dedicate more time to promoting the brand on social media.

F | Need to improve customer service by ensuring online orders are posted quickly.

(a) I would award 1 mark to B, E, and F because they are **Suggested answer** relevant impacts to Brad – that is, they are specific to his business.

(b) I would not award a mark to A, C, and D because they are **Suggested answer** generic answers – in other words, these points would be true of any business.

Hint
Remember, using the name of the character in the case study does not make your answer applicable. It has to be something specific to that business.

26

Mark the answer

1 Complete the student's answer so it would be awarded 2 marks.

6 (b) Outline **one** way that Brad meets customer needs. (2)

Hint
One way has been identified. The question asks you to 'outline' one way, so now you need to develop the answer to explain the stated method. You only need one step in your development.

Nearly there

He provides customers with a choice of goods. Meaning that

Suggested answer

customers can choose the styles and sizes that suit them.

2 Complete the student's answer so it would be awarded 2 marks.

6 (b) Outline **one** way that Brad meets customer needs. (2)

Hint
This time the supporting explanation has been identified, so you now need to identify the method being explained.

Nearly there

By providing his customers with a quality product.

Suggested answer

Meaning that his customers will be satisfied that their cycle wear will be durable.

I always try to leave time at the end of an exam to go back and check what I have written. Sometimes I find a silly mistake or realise I need to add another sentence to develop my explanation.

Connect the comments

1 Draw lines to connect the marker's comments to the relevant parts of the student's answer. One has been done for you. Some comments may relate to more than one sentence in the student's answer.

Hint
This is just the first paragraph of the student's answer; it is not the whole answer.

Brad is considering two options to expand his business.
Option 1: Add a range of running wear to his products.
Option 2: Open a store near the university.

6 (c) Justify which **one** of these two options Brad should choose. (9)

Had a go

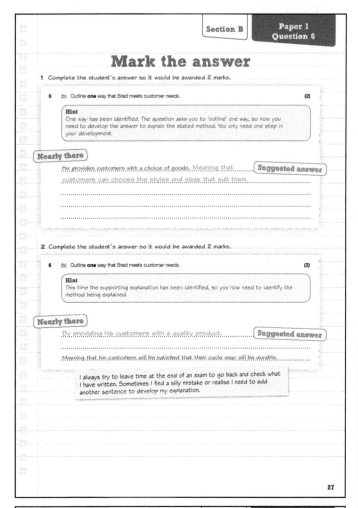

Brad should choose option 2 to open a new store.
This is because it will raise the profile of the business.
Being close to the university will mean that a lot of students will see his shop and go in. They will then want to buy his clothes because they are of good quality and reasonably priced. This means they will appeal to students as a target market. Sales will therefore increase. As more students see others wearing the cycle wear and also see the shop, awareness of the brand will grow further, leading to an increase in revenue.

- The student starts their answer with a clear judgement that option 2 should be chosen.

- The paragraph is then developed with a number of interconnected points showing a logical chain of reasoning.

- The judgement is then backed with a relevant argument.

- The student's argument is placed in context by considering the location of the store.

When planning my answers to the 9-mark 'Justify' questions, I go back to the case study and see whether I can find arguments for and against both options. I then decide which option I think is best before starting to write my answer. I can then tell the examiner what option I am going for in my opening sentence.

Find the answer

1 A student has written three paragraphs in response to the question on page 28. Their first paragraph is shown on page 28. One of the paragraphs below is to be the second paragraph in their answer.

(a) Which paragraph would you include as the second paragraph in the student's answer? Explain your choice.

(b) Then explain why you would **not** include the other two paragraphs.

Paragraph A

I wouldn't choose option 1 because Brad is a keen cyclist and building a brand for cycle wear. He is unlikely to know about running and might therefore design running gear that is not popular or fashionable because he does not understand the market. So he would waste a lot of money on research and development for a product that may not sell. Whereas we know he knows about cycle wear and has done market research, plus his brand is already known and liked by many cyclists.

Paragraph B

Another reason to open a shop near the university is because the land is likely to be cheaper than in a city centre. Therefore, he would be close to the market but with lower costs. This would help Brad to break even in the store quicker, as his fixed costs will be lower. He will therefore have a higher margin of safety. This means he will be able to make a profit based on a large number of students visiting his store and shopping there.

Paragraph C

However, opening a store will prove expensive. While operating via his website, Brad does not have high overhead costs such as rent and heating and lighting. A store would increase his fixed costs making it more difficult for Brad to make a profit. This is especially true as he may not make enough sales to cover costs. Students, who do not have a lot of money, may not want to buy cycle wear but rather make do with their everyday clothes. This may lead to Brad having cash flow problems as the cash coming in from sales may not be enough to cover his monthly cash outflows for rent and bills. This could lead to failure for Brad.

(a) I would include paragraph C because it provides balance to the **Suggested answer** answer by looking at the advantages and disadvantages of the chosen option.

(b) I would not include paragraph A and B because they do not **Suggested answer** provide balance. If option 2 is chosen and the advantages discussed in paragraph 1, discussing the disadvantages of the other option is not balanced – it is further support for the chosen option.

Mark the answer

Read the first two paragraphs of the student's answer on pages 28 and 29. Then read the student's final paragraph below, which is their conclusion to the question on page 28.
Use the mark scheme below to decide what mark you would give the student's answer as a whole. Justify your decision.

In conclusion, Brad should open a new store near the university because this will allow him to attract a large number of students into his store. They will be attracted by his reasonable prices and high quality, meaning his revenues will be high enough to cover his additional costs. However, this will depend upon him being able to find premises that are in a good location but not too expensive.

Level	Mark	Descriptor
	0	No rewardable material.
Level 1	1–3	• Limited application of knowledge and understanding of business concepts and issues to the business context (AO2). • Attempts to deconstruct business information and/or issues, finding limited connections between points (AO3a). • Makes a judgement, providing a simple justification based on limited evaluation of business information and issues relevant to the choice made (AO3b).
Level 2	4–6	• Sound application of knowledge and understanding of business concepts and issues to the business context, although there may be some inconsistencies (AO2). • Deconstructs business information and/or issues, finding interconnected points with chain of reasoning, although there may be some logical inconsistencies (AO3a). • Makes a judgement, providing a justification based on sound evaluation of business information and issues relevant to the choice made (AO3b).
Level 3	7–9	• Detailed application of knowledge and understanding of business concepts and issues to the business context throughout (AO2). • Deconstructs business information and/or issues, finding detailed interconnected points with logical chains of reasoning (AO3a). • Makes a judgement, providing a clear justification based on a thorough evaluation of business information and issues relevant to the choice made (AO3b).

I would give the student's answer 9 out of 9 marks because the student effectively weighs up the advantages and disadvantages of the chosen option before reaching a justified conclusion. The answer is well developed and in context throughout.

Panel 1 (page 32)

Paper 1 Question 7 | **Section C**

Find the answer

1 Find the answer that would be awarded 1 mark. Choose A, B or C. Explain your choice.

7 (a) State **one** stakeholder of Mr Nibs. (1)

Question	Answer	Mark
7 (a)	Award 1 mark for stating one stakeholder of Mr Nibs. Do not accept stakeholders that do not apply to Mr Nibs.	1

A   Shareholders

B   Suppliers

C   Employees

Hint
Read the question carefully and consider the context of the case study. Shareholders, suppliers and employees are all types of stakeholders, but which one is relevant to Mr Nibs?

Answer B would be awarded 1 mark because this is a correct stakeholder.

One of the suppliers to Mr Nibs is the cocoa farmers on the Ivory Coast.

Suggested answer

2 Find the answer that would be awarded 1 mark. Choose A, B or C. Explain your choice.

7 (a) State **one** type of ownership suitable to Mr Nibs. (1)

Question	Answer	Mark
7 (a)	Award 1 mark for stating one type of ownership suitable to Mr Nibs. Do not accept types of ownership that are not suitable to Mr Nibs.	1

A   Sole trader

B   Private limited company

C   Franchising

Suggested answer

Answer B would be awarded 1 mark because this is a suitable type of ownership.

Mr Nibs cannot be a sole trader when two people own the business.

Franchising is a way of starting up and running a business, it isn't a type

of ownership.

> When the command word is 'state', I try to answer the question in less than seven words. There is no need to write in complete sentences. This saves me time so that I do not run out of time on the higher mark questions.

32

Panel 2 (page 33)

Section C | **Paper 1 Question 7**

Complete the answer

1 Complete the student's answer so it would be awarded 2 marks.

Figure 2 shows the actual and forecast value of the chocolate market in £ millions.

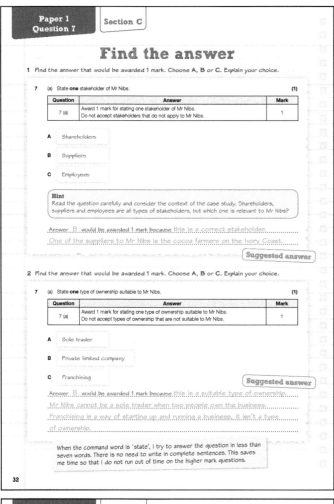

Figure 2

Hint
Remember that the information presented in graphs will be stated on each axis. It is important to read the axis carefully.

7 (b) Using **Figure 2**, calculate the forecast growth in the chocolate market from 2020 to 2021. (2)

2020 = 4620

2021 = 4710

4710 − 4620 = £90 million

2 Complete the student's answer so it would be awarded 2 marks.

7 (b) Using **Figure 2**, calculate the forecast growth in the chocolate market from 2017 to 2021. (2)

2017 = 4360

2021 = 4710

4710 − 4360 = £350 million

Hint
Always show your working out. This will help you to improve the quality of your response even if your answer is incorrect. It will prove that you have understood the process.

33

Panel 3 (page 34)

Paper 1 Question 7 | **Section C**

Complete the question

1 Complete the question by filling in the missing word or words.

7 (a) State **one** variable cost that Mr Nibs would have to pay. (1)

Nailed it!

Cocoa beans

2 Complete the question by filling in the missing word or words.

7 (a) State **one** fixed cost that Mr Nibs would have to pay. (1)

Nailed it!

Rent on the kitchen

3 Complete the question by filling in the missing word or words.

7 (a) State **one** cash inflow that Mr Nibs would show on the cash flow forecast. (1)

Nailed it!

Money from customers at food markets

4 Complete the question by filling in the missing word or words.

7 (a) State **one** customer need that Mr Nibs' customers would have. (1)

Nailed it!

Choice of flavour

5 Complete the question by filling in the missing word or words.

7 (a) State **one** competitor of Mr Nibs. (1)

Nailed it!

Other chocolatiers in York

> When I was revising, I made my own glossary of key terms to help remember what each term meant.

> When answering 1-mark questions, I try to ensure my answer is specific to the business and the products in the extract.

34

Panel 4 (page 35)

Section C | **Paper 1 Question 7**

Build the answer

1 Look at the question below and the list of ideas the student has extracted from the case study on page 31. The student has decided to choose option 2.
Which ideas (items A–J) would you use in a plan to answer this question? Tick the top five pieces of information you would use.

To increase profits Jock and Patricia are considering two options:
Option 1: Buying cheaper ingredients from different suppliers.
Option 2: Employing an assistant to attend food markets and maintain the website.

7 (d) Justify which **one** of these two options Mr Nibs should choose. (9)

Hint
Read through items A–J carefully before making your selection.

A	Their real passion was chocolate	☑
B	Set a social objective to only source the finest cocoa from the Ivory Coast	☐
C	To ensure farmers are paid a fair rate and well looked after	☐
D	Invest in a small commercial kitchen	☐
E	Still make all the chocolate themselves	☑
F	The two people attending all the food markets	☑
G	Buying the kitchen and equipment would cost £750 000	☑
H	Operates in a very competitive market	☐
I	There are big businesses operating in the market	☐
J	Confident that there is sufficient demand to continue to grow	☑

2 Look at the five items you have ticked. Choose **one** you would use in your argument for option 2. Justify your choice.

I would use item J because if the market is continuing to **[Suggested answer]**

grow then Mr Nibs should see an increase in demand in the future. They

will struggle to cope with this if they are still doing everything themselves.

Therefore, it is a good idea to employ an assistant.

35

Answers

Mark the answer

1 Use the mark scheme below to decide how many marks you would award the student's answer. Justify your decision.

To increase profits Jock and Patricia are considering two options:
Option 1: Buying cheaper ingredients from different suppliers.
Option 2: Employing an assistant to attend food markets and maintain the website.

7 (d) Justify which **one** of these two options Mr Nibs should choose. (9)

Jock and Patricia should choose option 1. By changing to a cheaper supplier for raw materials, such as cocoa, variable costs will go down. This will allow them to lower the price charged to customers. This is important because they operate in a competitive market with 10 independent chocolatiers in York. Therefore, they will attract more customers, increasing profit. However, this could damage the reputation of the brand. This is because they are no longer meeting the social objective of paying a fair rate to farmers. Overall, option 1 is the best because they do everything themselves and therefore shouldn't employ an assistant. This is a bad idea as it would raise costs and therefore lower profit.

Level	Mark	Descriptor
	0	No rewardable material.
Level 1	1–3	• Limited application of knowledge and understanding of business concepts and issues to the business context (AO2). • Attempts to deconstruct business information and/or issues, finding limited connections between points (AO3a). • Makes a judgement, providing a simple justification based on limited evaluation of business information and issues relevant to the choice made (AO3b).
Level 2	4–6	• Sound application of knowledge and understanding of business concepts and issues to the business context, although there may be some inconsistencies (AO2). • Deconstructs business information and/or issues, finding interconnected points with chain of reasoning, although there may be some logical inconsistencies (AO3a). • Makes a judgement, providing a justification based on sound evaluation of business information and issues relevant to the choice made (AO3b).
Level 3	7–9	• Detailed application of knowledge and understanding of business concepts and issues to the business context throughout (AO2). • Deconstructs business information and/or issues, finding detailed interconnected points with logical chains of reasoning (AO3a). • Makes a judgement, providing a clear justification based on a thorough evaluation of business information and issues relevant to the choice made (AO3b).

Suggested answer
I would award the student's answer 5 out of 9 marks because the student has a reasonable line of argument with sound application in the first paragraph. Unfortunately, however, the second paragraph is not developed. The third (concluding) paragraph does not offer balance...

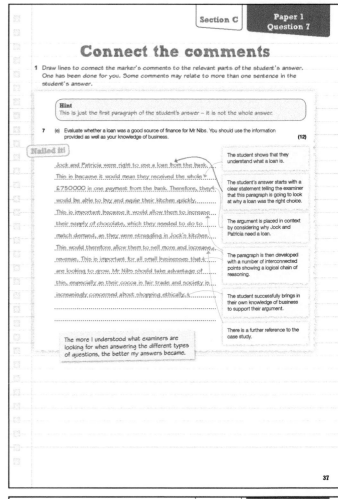

Connect the comments

1 Draw lines to connect the marker's comments to the relevant parts of the student's answer. One has been done for you. Some comments may relate to more than one sentence in the student's answer.

Hint
This is just the first paragraph of the student's answer – it is not the whole answer.

7 (e) Evaluate whether a loan was a good source of finance for Mr Nibs. You should use the information provided as well as your knowledge of business. (12)

Nailed it!

Jock and Patricia were right to use a loan from the bank. This is because it would mean they received the whole £750000 in one payment from the bank. Therefore, they would be able to buy and equip their kitchen quickly. This is important because it would allow them to increase their supply of chocolate, which they needed to do to match demand, as they were struggling in Jock's kitchen. This would therefore allow them to sell more and increase revenue. This is important for all small businesses that are looking to grow. Mr Nibs should take advantage of this, especially as their cocoa is fair trade and society is increasingly concerned about shopping ethically...

Comments:
- The student shows that they understand what a loan is.
- The student's answer starts with a clear statement telling the examiner that this paragraph is going to look at why a loan was the right choice.
- The argument is placed in context by considering why Jock and Patricia need a loan.
- The paragraph is then developed with a number of interconnected points showing a logical chain of reasoning.
- The student successfully brings in their own knowledge of business to support their argument.
- There is a further reference to the case study.

The more I understood what examiners are looking for when answering the different types of questions, the better my answers became.

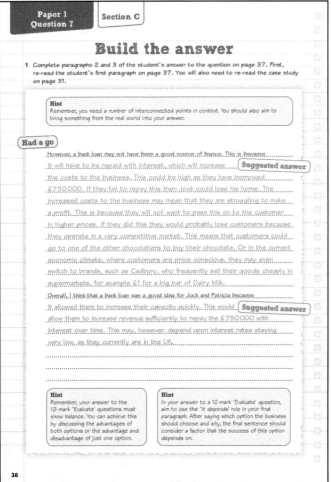

Build the answer

1 Complete paragraphs 2 and 3 of the student's answer to the question on page 37. First, re-read the student's first paragraph on page 37. You will also need to re-read the case study on page 31.

Hint
Remember, you need a number of interconnected points in context. You should also aim to bring something from the real world into your answer.

Had a go

However, a bank loan may not have been a good source of finance. This is because it will have to be repaid with interest, which will increase the costs to the business. This could be high as they have borrowed £750000. If they fail to repay this then Jock could lose his home. The increased costs to the business may mean that they are struggling to make a profit. This is because they will not want to pass this on to the customer in higher prices. If they did this they would probably lose customers because they operate in a very competitive market. This means that customers could go to one of the other chocolatiers to buy their chocolate. Or in the current economic climate, where customers are price conscious, they may even switch to brands, such as Cadbury, who frequently sell their goods cheaply in supermarkets, for example £1 for a big bar of Dairy Milk.
Overall, I think that a bank loan was a good idea for Jock and Patricia because it allowed them to increase their capacity quickly. This would allow them to increase revenue sufficiently to repay the £750000 with interest over time. This may, however, depend upon interest rates staying very low, as they currently are in the UK.

Hint
Remember, your answer to the 12-mark 'Evaluate' questions must show balance. You can achieve this by discussing the advantages of both options or the advantage and disadvantage of just one option.

Hint
In your answer to a 12-mark 'Evaluate' question, aim to use the 'it depends' rule in your final paragraph. After saying which option the business should choose and why, the final sentence should consider a factor that the success of this option depends on.

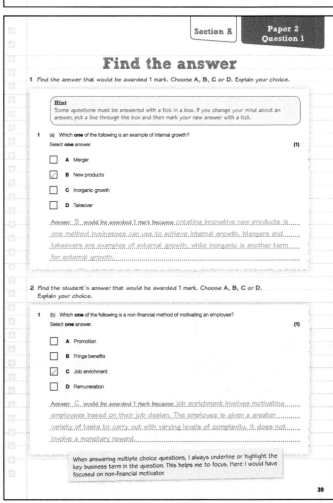

Find the answer

1 Find the answer that would be awarded 1 mark. Choose A, B, C or D. Explain your choice.

Hint
Some questions must be answered with a tick in a box. If you change your mind about an answer, put a line through the box and then mark your new answer with a tick.

1 (a) Which **one** of the following is an example of internal growth?
Select **one** answer. (1)

- [ ] A Merger
- [x] B New products
- [ ] C Inorganic growth
- [ ] D Takeover

Answer B would be awarded 1 mark because creating innovative new products is one method businesses can use to achieve internal growth. Mergers and takeovers are examples of external growth, while inorganic is another term for external growth.

2 Find the student's answer that would be awarded 1 mark. Choose A, B, C or D. Explain your choice.

1 (b) Which **one** of the following is a non-financial method of motivating an employee?
Select **one** answer. (1)

- [ ] A Promotion
- [ ] B Fringe benefits
- [x] C Job enrichment
- [ ] D Remuneration

Answer C would be awarded 1 mark because job enrichment involves motivating employees based on their job design. The employee is given a greater variety of tasks to carry out with varying levels of complexity. It does not involve a monetary reward.

When answering multiple choice questions, I always underline or highlight the key business term in the question. This helps me to focus. Here I would have focused on non-financial motivator.

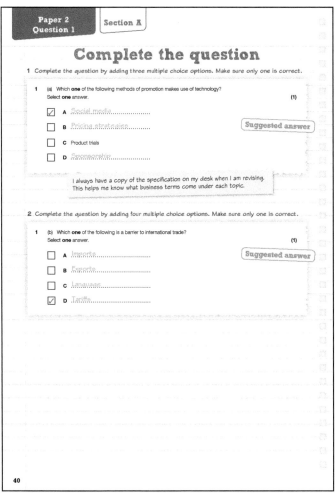

Complete the question

1 Complete the question by adding three multiple choice options. Make sure only one is correct.

1 (a) Which **one** of the following methods of promotion makes use of technology?
Select **one** answer. (1)

- ☑ **A** Social media
- ☐ **B** Pricing strategies
- ☐ **C** Product trials
- ☐ **D** Sponsorship

Suggested answer

> I always have a copy of the specification on my desk when I am revising. This helps me know what business terms come under each topic.

2 Complete the question by adding four multiple choice options. Make sure only one is correct.

1 (b) Which **one** of the following is a barrier to international trade?
Select **one** answer. (1)

- ☐ **A** Imports
- ☐ **B** Exports
- ☐ **C** Language
- ☑ **D** Tariffs

Suggested answer

Improve the answer

1 Use the hints below to write an improved answer to this question.

1 (c) Explain **one** benefit to a growing business of globalisation. (3)

> **Hint**
> Remember, for 3-mark 'Explain' questions there is 1 mark for stating a correct point, in this case a benefit. The further 2 marks are for explaining the benefit.

Had a go

Opportunity to sell overseas. This means that the business can reach a much larger target market, therefore increasing customer demand for its product and so increasing sales revenue.

Suggested answer

> **Hint**
> For this style of question, you need to make a relevant point followed by two strands in a line of argument. Use connectives such as 'this means that', 'therefore' and 'leading to' to help you develop your answer.

2 Use the hints below to write an improved answer to this question.

1 (d) Explain **one** drawback to a business of using job production. (3)

Nearly there

One drawback is that the rate at which goods are produced is likely to be slower. This is because each item is made individually to meet the needs of the customer. This means that costs, including labour costs, will be higher.

Suggested answer

Complete the answer

1 Complete the student's answer so it would be awarded 3 marks.

1 (c) Explain **one** drawback to a business of using loan capital as a source of finance. (3)

> **Hint**
> One drawback has been identified. The question asks you to 'explain' one drawback, so now you need to develop the answer to explain the disadvantage. Try to use two steps in your development.

Nearly there

One drawback is that the bank will charge interest. This means that the fixed costs of the business will be higher each month. Therefore, the business's net profit margin will be reduced.

Suggested answer

2 Complete the student's answer so it would be awarded 3 marks.

1 (d) Explain **one** impact of technology on human resources. (3)

> **Hint**
> This time the supporting explanation has been identified, so you now need to identify the impact being explained.

Nearly there

One impact is that employees will be able to work remotely. This will give them greater flexibility to work hours that suit from their own homes. As a result, employee motivation is likely to be higher.

Suggested answer

> I try to make sure that I use a business term in each sentence, so that my answers demonstrate my knowledge of the subject.

Mark the answer

1 A student has written an answer to this question. Use the marking instructions below to decide how many marks you would award the student's answer.

1 (c) Explain **one** benefit of a motivated workforce. (3)

One benefit is retaining employees. This means that they will stay with the business for longer. Therefore, recruitment costs will be lower.

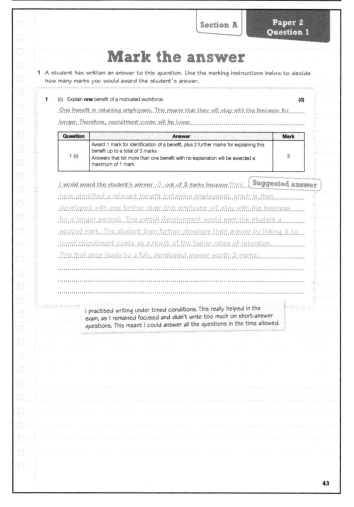

Question	Answer	Mark
1 (c)	Award 1 mark for identification of a benefit, plus 2 further marks for explaining this benefit up to a total of 3 marks. Answers that list more than one benefit with no explanation will be awarded a maximum of 1 mark.	3

I would award the student's answer 3 out of 3 marks because they have identified a relevant benefit (retaining employees), which is then developed with one further step (the employee will stay with the business for a longer period). This partial development would earn the student a second mark. The student then further develops their answer by linking it to lower recruitment costs as a result of the higher rates of retention. This final step leads to a fully developed answer worth 3 marks.

Suggested answer

> I practised writing under timed conditions. This really helped in the exam, as I remained focused and didn't write too much on short-answer questions. This meant I could answer all the questions in the time allowed.

Answers

Complete the question

1 Complete the question by adding three multiple choice options. Make sure two are correct.

> **Hint**
> Multiple choice questions often have answers that are believable but incorrect. These are called distractors. Try to make it relatively difficult to spot the incorrect answer.

2 (a) Which **two** of the following are phases in the product life cycle?
Select **two** answers. (2)

☐ A Market research
☐ B Design mix .... *Suggested answer*
☑ C Launch ....
☑ D Maturity ....
☐ E Market segmentation

2 Complete the question by adding three multiple choice options. Make sure two are correct.

2 (b) Which **two** of the following are benefits to a business of centralised decision-making?
Select **two** answers. (2)

☑ A Increased control by managers ......
☑ B Speeds up decision-making .... *Suggested answer*
☐ C Decision-making can be slow ....
☐ D Decisions shared with branches
☐ E Decision-makers may know their customers better

> My teacher gave me a copy of the specification for GCSE Business at the beginning of Year 10. It is a useful document to see what you need to know and it really helps me with revision.

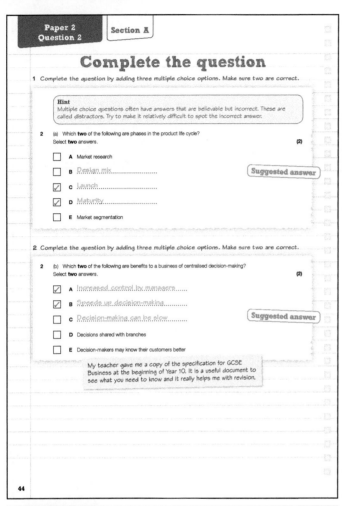

Mark the answer

1 Find the answers that would be awarded 2 marks. Choose two answers from A, B, C, D and E. Explain your choice.

> **Hint**
> Some questions must be answered with a tick in a box. If you change your mind about an answer, put a line through the box and then mark your new answer with a tick.

2 (a) Which **two** of the following are stages in the sales process?
Select **two** answers. (2)

☐ A Taking money
☐ B Quality control
☑ C Responses to customer feedback
☐ D Relationship with suppliers
☑ E Product knowledge

Answers C and E would be awarded 1 mark each because they are *Suggested answer*
stages in the sales process as listed on the Edexcel specification. Although
taking money may take place during a sales transaction, it is not listed as a
stage in the sales process.

2 Find the answer that would be awarded 2 marks. Choose two answers from A, B, C, D and E. Explain your choice.

2 (b) Which **two** of the following are documents used in the recruitment process?
Select **two** answers. (2)

☐ A Interviews
☑ B Person specification
☐ C Birth certificate
☑ D Application form
☐ E Attracting employees

> When revising processes or lists, I often draw them as a flow chart or spider diagram. This helps me to remember them, which means I feel more confident when answering multiple choice questions.

Answers B and D would be awarded 1 mark each because they are *Suggested answer*
documents used as part of the recruitment process as listed on the
Edexcel specification.

Find the answer

1 Find the student's answer that would be awarded 2 marks. Explain your choice.

Table 1 contains information about a business.

Cost of sales	£250000
Sales revenue	£480000
Other expenses	£120000

Table 1

2 (c) Using the information in **Table 1**, calculate the gross profit for the business. You are advised to show your workings. (2)

A $£480000 + £250000 = £730000$

B $£480000 - £250000 - £120000 = £110000$

C $\frac{£230000}{£480000} \times 100 = 48\%$

D $£250000 - £480000 = (£230000)$

E $\frac{£480000}{£250000} \times 100 = 19\%$

F $£480000 - £250000 = £230000$

G $£480000 + £250000 - £120000 = £610000$

Answer F would get 2 marks because to calculate gross profit *Suggested answer*
the formula is sales revenue − cost of sales.

> **Hint**
> Always show your workings. If you make a mistake but the examiner can see you were on the right track, you may still be awarded a mark.

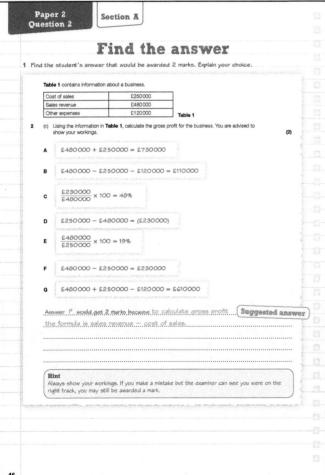

Complete the answer

1 Complete the student's answer below so that it would be awarded 2 marks.

Table 2 contains information about a business.

Gross profit	£980000
Sales revenue	£2500000
Net profit	£520000

Table 2

2 (c) Using the information in **Table 2**, calculate the gross profit margin for the business. You are advised to show your workings. (2)

> **Hint**
> In calculation questions, unless given specific instructions, it is a good idea to round a percentage up to a whole number.

Nearly there

$\frac{£980000}{£2500000} \times 100 = 39\%$

2 Complete the student's answer below so that it would be awarded 2 marks.

2 (c) Using the information in **Table 2** above, calculate the net profit margin for the business. You are advised to show your workings. (2)

Had a go

$\frac{£520000}{£2500000} \times 100 = 21\%$

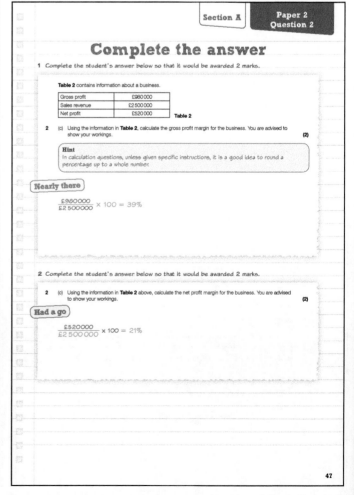

Complete the question

1 Complete the question by filling in the missing words.

> 2 (d) Explain **one** .... advantage .... to a business of making a ...... good supply ...... decision. **(3)**

Nailed it!

> Raw materials will be of the correct quality. Therefore, the business can produce a
> quality product. This will allow it to meet the needs of the customer.

2 Complete the question by filling in the missing words.

> 2 (d) Explain **one** ...... disadvantage ...... to a business of ...... internal recruitment ...... **(3)**

Nailed it!

> There may be a lack of new ideas brought into the business. This would mean that new
> processes are not introduced. This could lead to a loss of competitive advantage in
> the future.

> I always underline the key parts of the question before starting my answer.
> For example, for the 3-mark 'Explain' questions, I always check whether the
> question is asking for an advantage, disadvantage, impact or drawback.

Odd one out

1 Use the mark scheme below to decide which of these student answers would **not** be awarded 3 marks. Explain your decision.

> 2 (e) Explain **one** reason why a business might use market data to inform business decisions. **(3)**
>
> **Hint**
> Always read the question very carefully. Sometimes there are terms that are easy to confuse, such as 'market data' and 'marketing data'.

Question	Answer	Mark
2 (e)	Award 1 mark for identification of a reason, plus 2 further marks for explaining the reason up to a total of 3 marks.	3

A Market data will provide information about demographics. Therefore, the business will be able to identify a suitable target market. This will allow it to design goods to meet the needs of customers.

B One reason is to collect information on levels of customer satisfaction. This will allow a business to identify any weaknesses in its service. It can therefore make improvements to help build its reputation.

C Market data will indicate the size of the market to a business. This will allow it to better forecast sales. This means it will be able to plan how much of a product to produce to meet demand.

D One reason would be to identify the number of competitors. This would help indicate where there is opportunity for growth. This would help inform future plans for new outlets.

Answer B would **not** be awarded full marks because the answer **[Suggested answer]**
links to marketing data not market data. Therefore, it would be awarded no
marks for NAQ (not answering the question).

> I use a highlighter when reading the question to underline the business term.
> This helps me to make sure I am answering the precise question asked.

Find the answer

1 Find the answer that would be awarded 1 mark. Choose A, B, C or D. Explain your choice.

> **Hint**
> When answering a multiple choice question, it is important to read all of the options carefully.
> The examiner will often include an answer that is quite close to the correct one.
> If you cross through the answers you know are wrong first, this will help you to narrow down the correct answer.

3 (a) Which **one** of the following is an advantage of motivation?
Select **one** answer. **(1)**

- [ ] **A** Internal recruitment
- [✓] **B** Productivity
- [ ] **C** Flow production
- [ ] **D** Decentralisation

Answer B would be awarded 1 mark because a motivated **[Suggested answer]**
workforce will work harder, making them more productive. This will increase
levels of output per worker. This in turn would increase productivity.

2 Find the answer that would be awarded 1 mark. Choose A, B, C or D. Explain your choice.

3 (a) Which **one** of the following is an example of financial data that can be used to justify business decisions?
Select **one** answer. **(1)**

- [ ] **A** Customer opinions
- [ ] **B** Growth of market
- [✓] **C** Sales revenue
- [ ] **D** Demographics

> When answering multiple choice questions, I
> always read all of the answers before making
> my decision about which one is correct.

Answer C would be awarded 1 mark because sales revenue is the **[Suggested answer]**
finance coming into a business from sales.

Complete the question

1 Complete the question by filling in the missing words.

Table 3 contains information about a new machine that the business will keep for ... 3 ... years.

Total profit	£450 000
Cost ...... of new machine	£80 000

Table 3

3 (b) Using the information in **Table 3**, calculate the ... average ... rate of return for the new machine.
You are advised to ... show your workings ... **(2)**

Nailed it!

$$\frac{£450000}{3} = £150000$$

> **Hint**
> In calculation questions, unless given specific instructions, it is a good idea to round a percentage up to a whole number.

$$\frac{£150000}{£80000} \times 100 = 188\%$$

2 Complete the question by filling in the missing words.

Table 4 contains information about a business.

Cost ...... of sales	£400 000
Sales ... revenue ...	£650 000
Net ...... profit	£84 000

Table 4

3 (b) Using the information in **Table 4**, calculate the ... gross profit ...
You are advised to ... show your workings ... **(2)**

Nailed it!

£650 000 − £400 000 = £250 000

Complete the answer

1 Complete the student's answer so it would be awarded 3 marks.

> 3 (c) Explain **one** benefit to a business of training employees. (3)
>
> **Hint**
> One benefit has been identified. The question asks you to 'explain' one benefit, so now you need to develop the answer to explain the benefit. Try to use two steps in your development.

Nearly there

One benefit is that employees will have the necessary skills. **Suggested answer**
This means they will be able to carry out their job roles effectively,
leading to fewer mistakes.

2 Complete the student's answer so it would be awarded 3 marks.

> 3 (d) Explain **one** benefit to a business of using technology in production. (3)
>
> **Hint**
> This time the supporting explanation has been identified, so you now need to identify the impact being explained.

Nearly there

One benefit is increased speed of production. **Suggested answer**
This will allow the business to alter the number and types of goods produced.
Doing this means the business will be better able to respond to customer needs.

> I try to make sure that my first point uses the wording of the specification, so that the examiner knows I have understood all the topics.

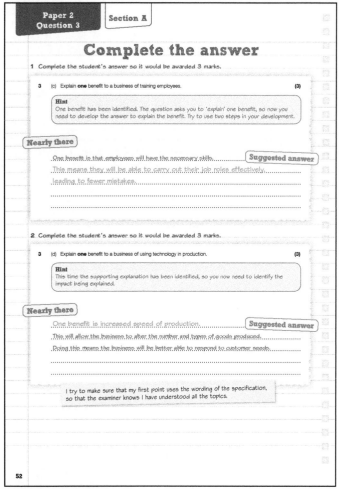

Mark the answer

1 A student has written an answer to this question. Use the marking instructions below to decide how many marks you would award the answer.

> 3 (c) Explain **one** impact of quality assurance. (3)
>
> One impact is that the business will have to employ a specialist to check the quality of a product once it has been made. This means that if there is a fault, it will only be picked up once the product is finished. This could lead to a large wastage cost.

Question	Answer	Mark
3 (c)	Award 1 mark for identification of an impact, plus 2 further marks for explaining this impact, up to a total of 3 marks. Answers that list more than one impact with no explanation will be awarded a maximum of 1 mark.	3

I would award this student's answer 0 out of 3 marks because they **Suggested answer** have discussed the impact of quality control, not quality assurance.

> In my notes I highlighted terms that were easily confused. This prompted me to consider the term in the question carefully before writing my answers. This helped me to avoid answering a question based on an incorrect starting point.

2 A student has written an answer to the following question. Choose which of the marker's comments it would be appropriate to use as feedback to the student.

> 3 (d) Explain **one** disadvantage to a business of behaving ethically. (3)

Nailed it!

One disadvantage is that costs to the business may be higher. This means that there will be a trade-off with profit. Therefore, the business may not be able to fund future growth.

A Well done, you have identified three relevant points to gain all 3 marks. ☐

B Good use of business terminology; however, I would like to see more strands to your argument. ☐

C One disadvantage identified and clearly explained with two strands in your development. ☑

D Good work, there are three clear strands in your answer. ☐

Re-order the answer

1 The sentences below are taken from a paragraph written by a student in response to the following question. Rearrange the sentences into the most logical order by numbering them 1 to 6.

> 3 (e) Discuss the benefit to a business of being ethical. (6)
>
> **Hint**
> It's important that answers to this type of question are in a logical order. Make sure you read your answer through from the start to check it makes sense.

Nailed it!

3 This will lead to repeat custom.

5 Consequently, the business will enjoy high sales while keeping its costs low.

1 One benefit is that stakeholders will recognise that the business is behaving in a way that people generally consider to be good.

6 This will allow the business to enjoy higher net profit margins.

2 Therefore, the business will gain a reputation for treating stakeholders well.

4 As a result, the business will need to spend less on advertising.

> When writing a longer response, I try to use a variety of phrases to help me build a developed argument, such as 'therefore', 'as a result', 'meaning that', etc.

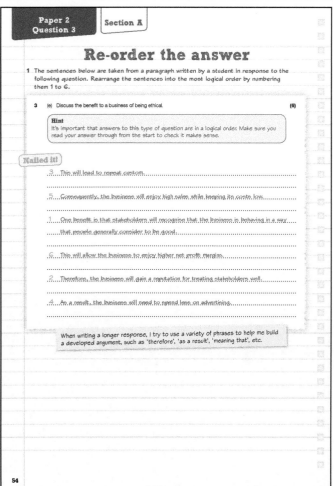

Connect the comments

1 Draw lines to connect the marker's comments to the relevant parts of the student's answer. One has been done for you. Some comments may relate to more than one sentence in the student's answer.

> 3 (e) Discuss the disadvantages to a business of being ethical. (6)

Had a go

Ethics is doing what is thought to be morally correct.
This can mean paying a fair wage to employees.
It can also mean paying more for supplies that are
from sustainable sources. This will reduce the profits
of a business.

- A correct disadvantage is given, but it is not clearly flagged up to the examiner as the main part of the argument.
- The student shows knowledge.
- The student jumps to the end of the argument without presenting a logical chain of reasoning.
- Examples are used to show understanding.

> When writing an extended answer, I try to remember to start with a relevant point and then fully develop this with a number of linked strands.

Hint
When a student makes a point that is relevant to the real world, rather than information taken from the extract, this is seen as showing their own knowledge of business.

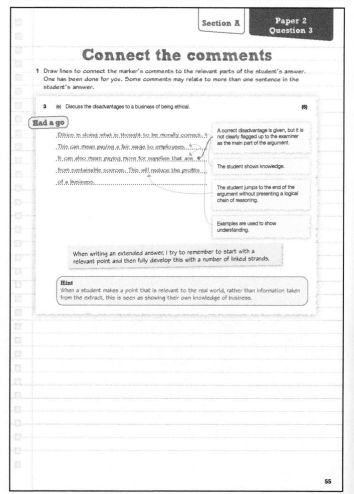

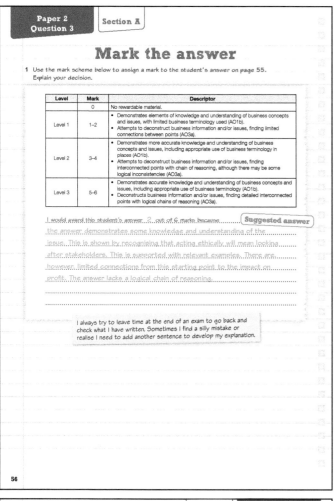

Paper 2 Question 3 | **Section A**

Mark the answer

1 Use the mark scheme below to assign a mark to the student's answer on page 55. Explain your decision.

Level	Mark	Descriptor
	0	No rewardable material.
Level 1	1–2	• Demonstrates elements of knowledge and understanding of business concepts and issues, with limited business terminology used (AO1b). • Attempts to deconstruct business information and/or issues, finding limited connections between points (AO3a).
Level 2	3–4	• Demonstrates more accurate knowledge and understanding of business concepts and issues, including appropriate use of business terminology in places (AO1b). • Attempts to deconstruct business information and/or issues, finding interconnected points with chain of reasoning, although there may be some logical inconsistencies (AO3a).
Level 3	5–6	• Demonstrates accurate knowledge and understanding of business concepts and issues, including appropriate use of business terminology (AO1b). • Deconstructs business information and/or issues, finding detailed interconnected points with logical chains of reasoning (AO3a).

I would award the student's answer 2 out of 6 marks because **Suggested answer** the answer demonstrates some knowledge and understanding of the issue. This is shown by recognising that acting ethically will mean looking after stakeholders. This is supported with relevant examples. There are, however, limited connections from this starting point to the impact on profit. The answer lacks a logical chain of reasoning.

> I always try to leave time at the end of an exam to go back and check what I have written. Sometimes I find a silly mistake or realise I need to add another sentence to develop my explanation.

56

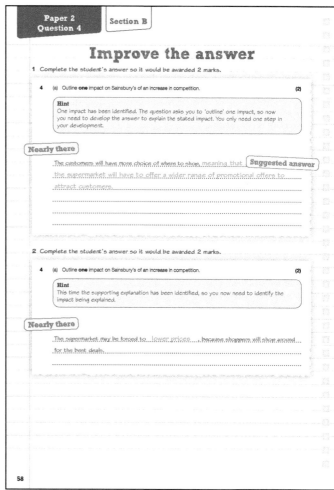

Paper 2 Question 4 | **Section B**

Improve the answer

1 Complete the student's answer so it would be awarded 2 marks.

4 (a) Outline **one** impact on Sainsbury's of an increase in competition. (2)

> **Hint**
> One impact has been identified. The question asks you to 'outline' one impact, so now you need to develop the answer to explain the stated impact. You only need one step in your development.

Nearly there

The customers will have more choice of where to shop, meaning that **Suggested answer** the supermarket will have to offer a wider range of promotional offers to attract customers.

2 Complete the student's answer so it would be awarded 2 marks.

4 (a) Outline **one** impact on Sainsbury's of an increase in competition. (2)

> **Hint**
> This time the supporting explanation has been identified, so you now need to identify the impact being explained.

Nearly there

The supermarket may be forced to lower prices because shoppers will shop around for the best deals.

58

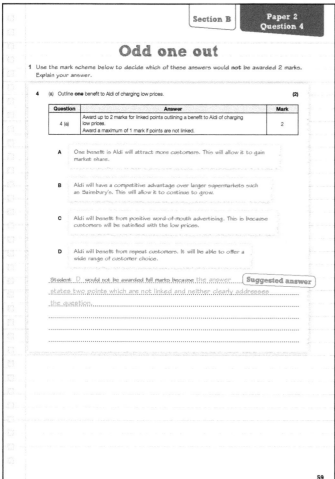

Section B | **Paper 2 Question 4**

Odd one out

1 Use the mark scheme below to decide which of these answers would **not** be awarded 2 marks. Explain your answer.

4 (a) Outline **one** benefit to Aldi of charging low prices. (2)

Question	Answer	Mark
4 (a)	Award up to 2 marks for linked points outlining a benefit to Aldi of charging low prices. Award a maximum of 1 mark if points are not linked.	2

A One benefit to Aldi will attract more customers. This will allow it to gain market share.

B Aldi will have a competitive advantage over larger supermarkets such as Sainsbury's. This will allow it to continue to grow.

C Aldi will benefit from positive word-of-mouth advertising. This is because customers will be satisfied with the low prices.

D Aldi will benefit from repeat customers. It will be able to offer a wide range of customer choice.

Student D would not be awarded full marks because the answer **Suggested answer** states two points which are not linked and neither clearly addresses the question.

59

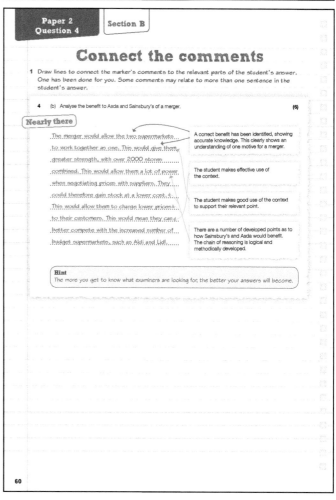

Paper 2 Question 4 | **Section B**

Connect the comments

1 Draw lines to connect the marker's comments to the relevant parts of the student's answer. One has been done for you. Some comments may relate to more than one sentence in the student's answer.

4 (b) Analyse the benefit to Asda and Sainsbury's of a merger. (6)

Nearly there

The merger would allow the two supermarkets to work together as one. This would give them greater strength, with over 2000 stores combined. This would allow them a lot of power when negotiating prices with suppliers. They could therefore gain stock at a lower cost. This would allow them to charge lower prices to their customers. This would mean they can better compete with the increased number of budget supermarkets, such as Aldi and Lidl.

A correct benefit has been identified, showing accurate knowledge. This clearly shows an understanding of one motive for a merger.

The student makes effective use of the context.

The student makes good use of the context to support their relevant point.

There are a number of developed points as to how Sainsbury's and Asda would benefit. The chain of reasoning is logical and methodically developed.

> **Hint**
> The more you get to know what examiners are looking for, the better your answers will become.

60

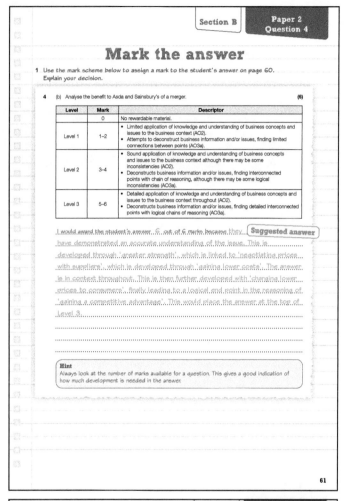

Mark the answer

1 Use the mark scheme below to assign a mark to the student's answer on page 60. Explain your decision.

4 (b) Analyse the benefit to Asda and Sainsbury's of a merger. (6)

Level	Mark	Descriptor
	0	No rewardable material.
Level 1	1–2	• Limited application of knowledge and understanding of business concepts and issues to the business context (AO2). • Attempts to deconstruct business information and/or issues, finding limited connections between points (AO3a).
Level 2	3–4	• Sound application of knowledge and understanding of business concepts and issues to the business context although there may be some inconsistencies (AO2). • Deconstructs business information and/or issues, finding interconnected points with chain of reasoning, although there may be some logical inconsistencies (AO3a).
Level 3	5–6	• Detailed application of knowledge and understanding of business concepts and issues to the business context throughout (AO2). • Deconstructs business information and/or issues, finding detailed interconnected points with logical chains of reasoning (AO3a).

I would award the student's answer 6 out of 6 marks because they *Suggested answer*
have demonstrated an accurate understanding of the issue. This is
developed through 'greater strength', which is linked to 'negotiating prices
with suppliers' which is developed through 'gaining lower costs'. The answer
is in context throughout. This is then further developed with 'changing lower
prices to consumers', finally leading to a logical end point in the reasoning of
'gaining a competitive advantage'. This would place the answer at the top of
Level 3.

Hint
Always look at the number of marks available for a question. This gives a good indication of how much development is needed in the answer.

61

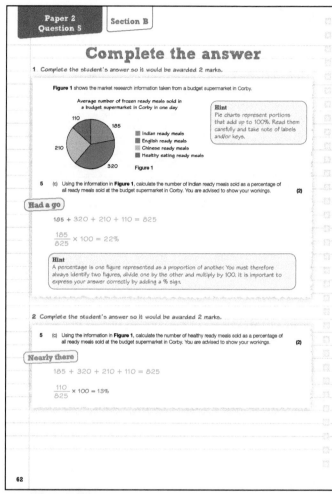

Complete the answer

1 Complete the student's answer so it would be awarded 2 marks.

Figure 1 shows the market research information taken from a budget supermarket in Corby.

Average number of frozen ready meals sold in a budget supermarket in Corby in one day

110 · 185 · 210 · 320

■ Indian ready meals
■ English ready meals
☐ Chinese ready meals
■ Healthy eating ready meals

Figure 1

Hint
Pie charts represent portions that add up to 100%. Read them carefully and take note of labels and/or keys.

5 (c) Using the information in **Figure 1**, calculate the number of Indian ready meals sold as a percentage of all ready meals sold at the budget supermarket in Corby. You are advised to show your workings. (2)

Had a go

185 + 320 + 210 + 110 = 825

$\frac{185}{825} \times 100 = 22\%$

Hint
A percentage is one figure represented as a proportion of another. You must therefore always identify two figures, divide one by the other and multiply by 100. It is important to express your answer correctly by adding a % sign.

2 Complete the student's answer so it would be awarded 2 marks.

5 (c) Using the information in **Figure 1**, calculate the number of healthy ready meals sold as a percentage of all ready meals sold at the budget supermarket in Corby. You are advised to show your workings. (2)

Nearly there

185 + 320 + 210 + 110 = 825

$\frac{110}{825} \times 100 = 13\%$

62

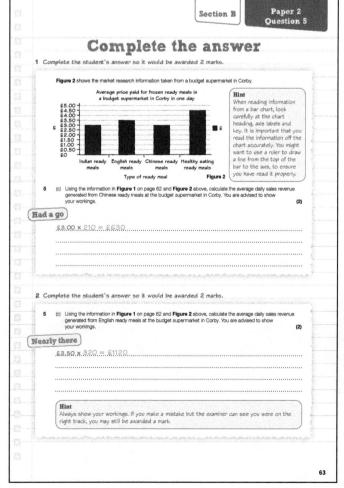

Complete the answer

1 Complete the student's answer so it would be awarded 2 marks.

Figure 2 shows the market research information taken from a budget supermarket in Corby.

Average price paid for frozen ready meals in a budget supermarket in Corby in one day

£5.00, £4.50, £4.00, £3.50, £3.00, £2.50, £2.00, £1.50, £1.00, £0.50, £0

Indian ready meals · English ready meals · Chinese ready meals · Healthy eating ready meals

Type of ready meal **Figure 2**

Hint
When reading information from a bar chart, look carefully at the chart heading, axis labels and key. It is important that you read the information off the chart accurately. You might want to use a ruler to draw a line from the top of the bar to the axis, to ensure you have read it properly.

5 (c) Using the information in **Figure 1** on page 62 and **Figure 2** above, calculate the average daily sales revenue generated from Chinese ready meals at the budget supermarket in Corby. You are advised to show your workings. (2)

Had a go

£3.00 × 210 = £630

2 Complete the student's answer so it would be awarded 2 marks.

5 (c) Using the information in **Figure 1** on page 62 and **Figure 2** above, calculate the average daily sales revenue generated from English ready meals at the budget supermarket in Corby. You are advised to show your workings. (2)

Nearly there

£3.50 × 320 = £1120

Hint
Always show your workings. If you make a mistake but the examiner can see you were on the right track, you may still be awarded a mark.

63

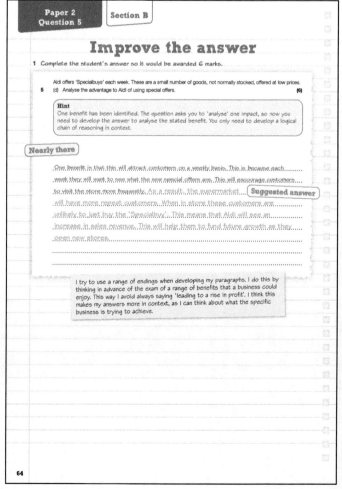

Improve the answer

1 Complete the student's answer so it would be awarded 6 marks.

Aldi offers 'Specialbuys' each week. These are a small number of goods, not normally stocked, offered at low prices.

5 (d) Analyse the advantage to Aldi of using special offers. (6)

Hint
One benefit has been identified. The question asks you to 'analyse' one impact, so now you need to develop the answer to analyse the stated benefit. You only need to develop a logical chain of reasoning in context.

Nearly there

One benefit is that this will attract customers on a weekly basis. This is because each
week they will want to see what the new special offers are. This will encourage customers
to visit the store more frequently. As a result, the supermarket *Suggested answer*
will have more repeat customers. When in store these customers are
unlikely to just buy the 'Specialbuy'. This means that Aldi will see an
increase in sales revenue. This will help them to fund future growth as they
open new stores.

Had a go
I try to use a range of endings when developing my paragraphs. I do this by thinking in advance of the exam of a range of benefits that a business could enjoy. This way I avoid always saying 'leading to a rise in profit'. I think this makes my answers more in context, as I can think about what the specific business is trying to achieve.

64

Panel 1 (page 65)

Section B | Paper 2 Question 6

Mark the answer

1 Find the correct answer. Choose A, B or C. Explain your choice.

6 (a) State **one** influence on the pricing strategy used by Aldi. (1)

Question	Answer	Mark
6 (a)	Award 1 mark for stating one influence on the pricing strategy used by Aldi. Do not accept strategies that do not apply to Aldi.	1

A Low price

B High price

C Market segments

Answer ..C.. would be awarded 1 mark because this is an influence **[Suggested answer]** on a pricing strategy. Aldi is influenced by the market segment it targets. The question did not ask for the strategy used, which is low price.

2 Find the correct answer. Choose A, B or C. Explain your choice.

6 (a) State **one** way of working for sales assistants at Aldi. (1)

Question	Answer	Mark
6 (a)	Award 1 mark for stating one way of working for sales assistants at Aldi. Do not accept ways that are not suitable to Aldi.	1

A Freelance contracts

B Part-time

C Remote working

Answer ..B.. would be awarded 1 mark because this is a suitable way **[Suggested answer]** of sales assistants working at Aldi. Sales assistants need to be in store and therefore cannot work remotely. Nor would it be suitable in these job roles to employ freelance contractors.

> When the command word is 'state', I try to answer the question using as few words as possible. There is no need to write in complete sentences. This saves me time so that I can make sure I do not run out of time on the higher mark questions.

65

Panel 2 (page 66)

Paper 2 Question 6 | Section B

Improve the answer

1 Complete the student's answer so it would be awarded 2 marks.

6 (b) Outline **one** advantage to Tesco of being a public limited company (PLC). (2)

> **Hint**
> One advantage has been identified. The question asks you to 'outline' one advantage, so now you need to develop the answer to explain the stated advantage. You only need one step in your development.

[Nearly there]

As a PLC Tesco will be considered to be more prestigious and reliable. This means that it will be in a stronger position to negotiate **[Suggested answer]** deals with suppliers, such as farmers.

2 Complete the student's answer so it would be awarded 2 marks.

6 (b) Outline **one** advantage to Tesco of being a public limited company (PLC). (2)

> **Hint**
> This time the supporting explanation has been identified, so you now need to identify the advantage being explained.

[Nearly there]

One advantage is that Tesco will be seen as a prestigious **[Suggested answer]** company. Therefore, it will have more power when negotiating with suppliers who want to be stocked by the supermarket.

66

Panel 3 (page 67)

Section B | Paper 2 Question 6

Build the answer

1 Look at the question and the list of ideas the student has extracted from the case study on page 57. The student has decided to choose option 1. Which ideas would you use in a plan to answer this question? Tick your top six pieces of information.

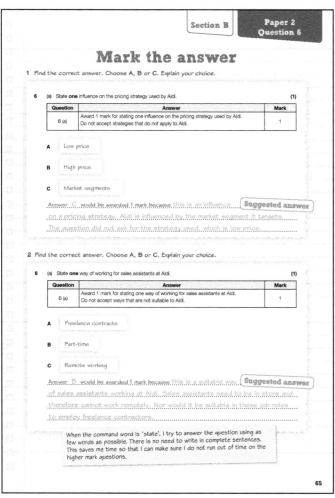

To achieve an objective of growth Bonjour is considering two options:
Option 1: Opening smaller stores in city centres
Option 2: Offering an e-commerce option allowing customers to have their shopping delivered

6 (c) Justify which **one** of these two options Bonjour should choose. (9)

> **Hint**
> Read through items A–I carefully before making your selection.

A Tesco is a large competitor. ☐

B This format has proved successful for larger supermarkets such as Tesco. ☑

C Building an e-commerce site would be expensive. ☐

D Consumers are increasingly looking for convenience. ☑

E Aldi has just started doing this so Bonjour could follow the trend. ☑

F Bonjour is new on the market but could use this to achieve growth. ☑

G Bonjour is French. ☐

H By locating in city centres, Bonjour could quickly become recognised even though it is new to the market. ☑

I Bonjour sells a range of fresh produce such as breads and cakes cooked in store. ☑

2 Look at the items you have ticked. Choose **one** you would use in your argument **for** option 1. Justify your choice.

H. Bonjour would have a high footfall if it located in the city centre. This means that even though it does not yet have brand recognition, customers would visit it as it offers convenience. This would allow it to become established in the UK market more quickly.

> **Hint**
> It is useful to note the number of marks a question is worth and break down your time accordingly.

67

Panel 4 (page 68)

Paper 2 Question 6 | Section B

Mark the answer

1 Use the mark scheme below to decide what mark you would give the student's answer to the question on page 67. Justify your decision.

Bonjour should open smaller stores in city centres. They are new to the UK market and this would allow them high visibility. This would mean that customers would try the new store when looking to buy food from a convenient location. Therefore, Bonjour would quickly gain a good reputation. This is because customers who try the freshly baked cakes are likely to go back, therefore allowing Bonjour to quickly gain a reputation. This could give them a competitive advantage over rivals Aldi.

Setting up a new e-commerce site is likely to be expensive. This is because Bonjour would have to build a website, buy delivery vans and employ drivers. It is unlikely that Bonjour would be able to compete against large competitors, such as Tesco, who already offer a delivery service. Therefore, this option would prove costly and is likely to fail.

Overall option 1 is the best, because it will allow Bonjour to achieve its objective of growth. The main reason for this is because customers who try the freshly baked goods are likely to become loyal to the brand.

Level	Mark	Descriptor
	0	No rewardable material.
Level 1	1–3	• Limited application of knowledge and understanding of business concepts and issues to the business context (AO2). • Attempts to deconstruct business information and/or issues, finding limited connections between points (AO3a). • Makes a judgement, providing a simple justification based on limited evaluation of business information and issues relevant to the choice made (AO3b).
Level 2	4–6	• Sound application of knowledge and understanding of business concepts and issues to the business context, although there may be some inconsistencies (AO2). • Deconstructs business information and/or issues, finding interconnected points with chain of reasoning, although there may be some logical inconsistencies (AO3a). • Makes a judgement, providing a justification based on sound evaluation of business information and issues relevant to the choice made (AO3b).
Level 3	7–9	• Detailed application of knowledge and understanding of business concepts and issues to the business context throughout (AO2). • Deconstructs business information and/or issues, finding detailed interconnected points with logical chains of reasoning (AO3a). • Makes a judgement, providing a clear justification based on a thorough evaluation of business information and issues relevant to the choice made (AO3b).

I would give this answer ..4.. out of 9 marks because the student **[Suggested answer]** has a reasonable line of argument with sound application in the first paragraph. Unfortunately, however, the second paragraph does not provide balance. Presenting an argument against the dismissed option only supports the chosen option. To provide balance, the second paragraph should be against the chosen option or for the dismissed option. It is difficult to make a fully justified recommendation when the argument is not balanced.

68

Answers

Find the answer

1 Find the student's answer that would be awarded 1 mark. Choose A, B, C or D. Explain your choice.

7 (a) Define the term private limited company. (1)

A   A company that can sell shares on a stock exchange

B   A company that sells a range of goods to members of the public

C   A company that can sell shares to family and friends

D   A company that is owned by just one person

Answer: C would be awarded 1 mark because a private limited company is one that cannot advertise shares for sale to the general public but can sell them to people known to the company. It can, therefore, sell shares to family and friends.

2 Find the student's answer that would be awarded 1 mark. Choose A, B, C or D. Explain your choice.

7 (a) Define the term sponsorship. (1)

A   Providing financial support for an event in return for brand exposure

B   Paying a sports person to compete in a high profile event

C   Advertising a brand in the media

D   A promotional method used to raise awareness of a brand

Answer: A would be awarded one mark because sponsorship takes place when a business provides financial support for an event or good cause. In return, the profile of the business is raised due to the name or logo being advertised at the event, for example on clothing, display boards or in a programme.

70

Find the answer

Find the answer

1 Find the student's answer that would be awarded 1 mark. Choose A, B or C. Explain your choice.

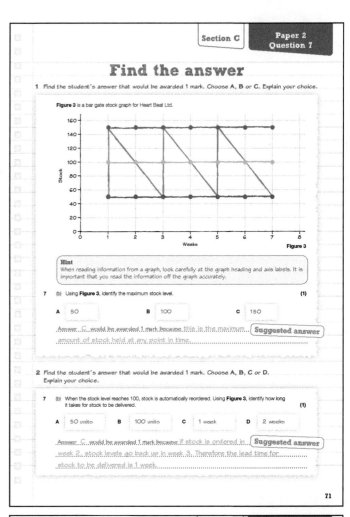

Figure 3 is a bar gate stock graph for Heart Beat Ltd.

Hint
When reading information from a graph, look carefully at the graph heading and axis labels. It is important that you read the information off the graph accurately.

7 (b) Using **Figure 3**, identify the maximum stock level. (1)

A   50   B   100   C   150

Answer: C would be awarded 1 mark because this is the maximum [Suggested answer] amount of stock held at any point in time.

2 Find the student's answer that would be awarded 1 mark. Choose A, B, C or D. Explain your choice.

7 (b) When the stock level reaches 100, stock is automatically reordered. Using **Figure 3**, identify how long it takes for stock to be delivered. (1)

A   50 units   B   100 units   C   1 week   D   2 weeks

Answer: C would be awarded 1 mark because if stock is ordered in [Suggested answer] week 2, stock levels go back up in week 3. Therefore the lead time for stock to be delivered is 1 week.

71

Connect the comments

1 Draw lines to connect the marker's comments to the relevant parts of the student's answer. One has been done for you. Some comments may relate to more than one sentence in the student's answer.

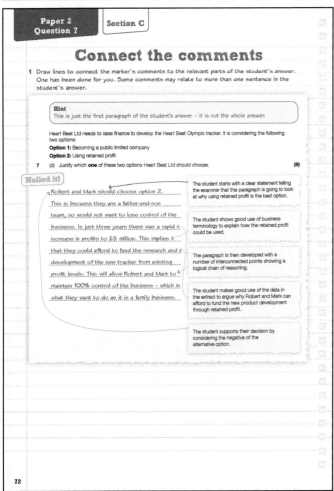

Hint
This is just the first paragraph of the student's answer – it is not the whole answer.

Heart Beat Ltd needs to raise finance to develop the Heart Beat Olympic tracker. It is considering the following two options:
Option 1: Becoming a public limited company
Option 2: Using retained profit

7 (d) Justify which **one** of these two options Heart Beat Ltd should choose. (9)

[Nailed it!]

Robert and Mark should choose option 2. This is because they are a father-and-son team, so would not want to lose control of the business. In just three years there was a rapid increase in profits to £5 million. This implies that they could afford to fund the research and development of the new tracker from existing profit levels. This will allow Robert and Mark to maintain 100% control of the business – which is what they want to do as it is a family business.

The student starts with a clear statement telling the examiner that this paragraph is going to look at why using retained profit is the best option.

The student shows good use of business terminology to explain how the retained profit could be used.

The paragraph is then developed with a number of interconnected points showing a logical chain of reasoning.

The student makes good use of the data in the extract to argue why Robert and Mark can afford to fund the new product development through retained profit.

The student supports their decision by considering the negative of the alternative option.

72

Re-order the answer

1 The sentences below are taken from a paragraph written by a student in response to the following question. Rearrange the sentences into the most logical order by numbering them 1 to 8.

7 (e) Evaluate the importance of quality to Heart Beat Ltd. You should use the information provided as well as your knowledge of business. (12)

Hint
It's important that answers to this type of question are in a logical order. Make sure you read your answer through from the start to check it makes sense.

5   Otherwise, there will be complaints.

1   Quality is important to Heart Beat because a poor-quality product could damage its reputation.

8   This would be very dangerous, as this is a competitive market with big businesses such as Apple and Fitbit, that have a large share of the market.

2   This is especially true as Heart Beat is bringing out a luxury version of its fitness tracker.

7   Leading to a loss of their competitive advantage.

3   Therefore, to warrant a high price of £249 it will have to be of good quality.

4   This means that it must fulfil all of the functions such as allowing emails effectively.

6   This would mean that other businesses such as the insurance company, would not want to work with them.

When I read the extract, I try to identify other businesses that I know operate in the same market. This helps me bring my own knowledge of business into my answers.

73

Mark the answer

1 Use the mark scheme below to decide what mark you would give the student's answer. Justify your decision. The whole answer is the rearranged answer on page 73 plus the following two paragraphs. Look back at page 73 to remind yourself of the main points.

7 (e) Evaluate the importance of quality to Heart Beat Ltd. You should use the information provided as well as your knowledge of business. **(12)**

Hint
12-mark 'Evaluate' questions require an extended response with a number of steps in a line of reasoning on context. It is important to try to use business terminology within your line of reasoning as well as specific information from the extract provided. The analytical paragraphs should lead to a fully supported conclusion based on the context provided.

Quality is also important, as this will allow Heart Beat to control costs. This in an important part of the design mix alongside function and aesthetics. If there are quality issues then goods will be faulty, leading to high wastage costs to either scrap or make the trackers. This would push costs up, meaning that Heart Beat would see a fall in profit margins. Their Heart Beat Olympic tracker is competitively priced at £249, which is cheaper than rivals who charge £350. This is an important competitive advantage to Heart Beat, who may not have the brand loyalty of other businesses in the market. This is important, as Heart Beat may be targeting customers who cannot afford the alternatives. These customers are more aware of prices and would also be attracted by the discount on the life insurance. This could be especially true in the UK at the moment, where there are high levels of uncertainty about the economy. Overall, I think quality is very important to Heart Beat. The main reason for this is that customers will want a product that lasts and can be trusted to carry out all of the functions that Heart Beat says it does.

Level	Mark	Descriptor
	0	No rewardable material.
Level 1	1–4	• Demonstrates elements of knowledge and understanding of business concepts and issues, with limited business terminology used (AO1b). • Limited application of knowledge and understanding of business concepts and issues to the business context (AO2). • Attempts to deconstruct business information and/or issues, finding limited connections between points (AO3a). • Draws a conclusion, supported by generic assertions from limited evaluation of business information and issues (AO3b).
Level 2	5–8	• Demonstrates mostly accurate knowledge and understanding of business concepts and issues, including appropriate use of business terminology in places (AO1b). • Sound application of knowledge and understanding of business concepts and issues to the business context, although there may be some inconsistencies (AO2). • Deconstructs business information and/or issues, finding interconnected points with chains of reasoning, although there may be some logical inconsistencies (AO3a). • Draws a conclusion based on sound evaluation of business information and issues (AO3b).
Level 3	9–12	• Demonstrates accurate knowledge and understanding of business concepts and issues throughout, including appropriate use of business terminology (AO1b). • Detailed application of knowledge and understanding of business concepts and issues to the business context throughout (AO2). • Deconstructs business information and/or issues, finding detailed interconnected points with logical chains of reasoning (AO3a). • Draws a valid and well-reasoned conclusion based on a thorough evaluation of business information and issues (AO3b).

I would give the student's answer 9 out of 12 marks because the **Suggested answer** student has a reasonable line of argument with sound application in the first and second paragraphs. Both paragraphs have a number of interconnected points showing a logical chain of reasoning and effective use of the context. In both paragraphs the student tries to bring in some of their own knowledge of business. Unfortunately, the conclusion lacks justification, keeping the answer at the bottom of Level 3.

Published by Pearson Education Limited, 80 Strand, London, WC2R 0RL.

www.pearsonschoolsandfecolleges.co.uk

Copies of official specifications for all Pearson qualifications may be found on the website:
qualifications.pearson.com

Text and illustrations © Pearson Education Ltd 2020
Typeset and illustrated by Kamae Design
Produced by Newgen Publishing UK
Cover illustration by Eoin Coveney

The right of Helen Coupland-Smith to be identified as author of this work has been asserted
by her in accordance with the Copyright, Designs and Patents Act 1988.

First published 2020

24
10 9 8 7 6 5 4 3 2

British Library Cataloguing in Publication Data
A catalogue record for this book is available from the British Library

ISBN 978 1 292 29666 1

Copyright notice
All rights reserved. No part of this publication may be reproduced in any form or by
any means (including photocopying or storing it in any medium by electronic means and
whether or not transiently or incidentally to some other use of this publication) without
the written permission of the copyright owner, except in accordance with the provisions
of the Copyright, Designs and Patents Act 1988 or under the terms of a licence issued
by the Copyright Licensing Agency, Hay's Galleria, Shackleton House, 4 Battle Bridge
Lane, London SE1 2HX (www.cla.co.uk). Applications for the copyright owner's written
permission should be addressed to the publisher.

Printed by CPI Group (UK) Ltd, Croydon CR0 4YY

Acknowledgements
We would like to thank Joni Sommerville, Theo Mellors, Emily Plenty, John-Paul Duddy,
Emily Atkinson, Jess Salmon, Holly Coop, Matthew Foot and David Birch for their
invaluable help in providing student tips for the series.

Notes from the publisher
1. While the publishers have made every attempt to ensure that advice on the qualification
and its assessment is accurate, the official specification and associated assessment guidance
materials are the only authoritative source of information and should always be referred to
for definitive guidance.
Pearson examiners have not contributed to any sections in this resource relevant to
examination papers for which they have responsibility.

2. Pearson has robust editorial processes, including answer and fact checks, to ensure the
accuracy of the content in this publication, and every effort is made to ensure this publication
is free of errors. We are, however, only human, and occasionally errors do occur. Pearson is
not liable for any misunderstandings that arise as a result of errors in this publication, but it
is our priority to ensure that the content is accurate. If you spot an error, please do contact us
at resourcescorrections@pearson.com so we can make sure it is corrected.